EMIL BRUNNER'S INTEGRATION OF FAITH AND REASON

EMIL BRUNNER'S INTEGRATION OF FAITH AND REASON

Modern Perspectives on Religious-Philosophical Methods and Natural Theology

DONG IN BAEK

◥PICKWICK *Publications* • Eugene, Oregon

EMIL BRUNNER'S INTEGRATION OF FAITH AND REASON
Modern Perspectives on Religious-Philosophical Methods and Natural Theology

Copyright © 2024 Dong In Baek. All rights reserved. Except for brief quotations in critical publications or reviews, no part of this book may be reproduced in any manner without prior written permission from the publisher. Write: Permissions, Wipf and Stock Publishers, 199 W. 8th Ave., Suite 3, Eugene, OR 97401.

Pickwick Publications
An Imprint of Wipf and Stock Publishers
199 W. 8th Ave., Suite 3
Eugene, OR 97401

www.wipfandstock.com

PAPERBACK ISBN: 978-1-6667-8207-3
HARDCOVER ISBN: 978-1-6667-8208-0
EBOOK ISBN: 978-1-6667-8209-7

Cataloguing-in-Publication data:

Names: Baek, Dong In, author.

Title: Emil Brunner's integration of faith and reason : modern perspectives on religious-philosophical methods and natural theology / Dong In Baek.

Description: Eugene, OR : Pickwick Publications, 2024 | Includes bibliographical references and index.

Identifiers: ISBN 978-1-6667-8207-3 (paperback) | ISBN 978-1-6667-8208-0 (hardcover) | ISBN 978-1-6667-8209-7 (ebook)

Subjects: LCSH: Brunner, Emil, 1889–1966. | Faith and reason. | Revelation. | Christian ethics—Controversial literature. | Rationalism. | Faith and reason—Christianity. | Revelation—Christianity

Classification: BT127 .B20 2024 (paperback) | BT127 .B20 (ebook)

05/02/24

English translations of German passages are the author's original translation.

To Professor Jürgen Moltmann, my esteemed mentor, whose theological insights and dedication to hope have guided many, this work is dedicated.

CONTENTS

Preface | xi

Prologue | xiii

Introduction: Problem and Method | 1

First Part: Brunner's Understanding of Religious Knowledge and Symbolism as the Origin of Religion in His Early Period (1914) | 4

    1.1. Religion: Knowledge or Experience? | 4

    1.2. The Intuition for Religious Knowledge | 8

    1.3. Religious Knowledge in Addition to Intuition | 13

    1.4. The Concept of Religious Knowledge: "Spiritual Supra-world" and "Supra-Human Personality" | 16

    1.5. The Symbolic Understanding of God through Religious Knowledge | 21

        1.5.1. The Sign and Expression Function of Symbols | 21

        1.5.2. The Symbolization of Religious Knowledge | 24

    1.6. Summary: Religious Knowledge and Symbol | 27

Second Part: Brunner's Theological Development after 1921 | 31

    2.1. Transformation to Dialectical Theology | 31

        2.1.1. Brunner's Transition to Dialectics | 31

2.1.2. Brunner's Concept of Faith Based on the Analogy between God and Humans: Theology of the Word | 36

    2.1.2.1. The Relationship between Faith and Psychology | 36

    2.1.2.2. The Relationship of Faith to History | 39

2.1.3. The Theological Position of Emil Brunner during This Period | 44

2.2. Brunner's Theological Arguments between General and Special Revelation (1927) | 47

    2.2.1. Assumption of Thought | 47

    2.2.2. The Possibility of Knowledge of God through Revelation in Nature | 48

    2.2.3. Brunner's Critique of the Understanding of Special Revelation in "Contemporary Modern Theology" | 54

2.3. Turn to Eristic (1928) | 61

    2.3.1. Continuity in Brunner's Thinking | 61

    2.3.2. The Transformation to the I-Thou Philosophy | 65

    2.3.3. The New Path towards the "Other Task of Theology" | 71

Third Part: Brunner's View of Modern Natural Theology | 78

3.1. Premise of Thought | 78

3.2. The Possibility of an Unbroken Connection between God and Humanity as a Root of the Concept of Revelation | 83

3.3. Das neue Menschenverständnis in Wahrheit als Begegnung | 86

    3.3.1. The Human Being in the Contradiction of Creation and Sin | 86

    3.3.2. The Restoration of Imago Dei as an "Everlasting Revelation Event" | 90

3.4. The True Personal Encounter | 94

Conclusion: Results and Outlook | 96

Epilogue: A Final Reflection on Emil Brunner and His Impact on Religious-Philosophical Method | 103

About the Author | 109

Bibliography | 111

Index | 119

PREFACE

ESTEEMED READER,

In your hands now rests *Emil Brunner's Integration of Faith and Reason: Modern Perspectives on Religious-Philosophical Methods and Natural Theology*, a scholarly work born from my intricate journey into the labyrinth of natural theology and its subsequent philosophical confrontations.

At the dawn of this intellectual pilgrimage, the formidable figure of Professor Jürgen Moltmann stands tall. His seminal work, *Theology of Hope*, kindled within me a spark that would grow into a guiding light. Under his enlightening influence, I enthusiastically immersed myself in the fascinating dialectic between Karl Barth and Emil Brunner. I am deeply indebted to Professor Moltmann for providing the vast canvas upon which the thoughts and ideas of this book could be sketched, offering the "big picture" that made this exploration of natural theology possible.

To my wife Eunhye, whose unwavering faith in me has endured even the darkest times, I owe an immeasurable debt of gratitude. Emma, whose superior skills in translation were instrumental, has breathed life into my words with her deft touch and deep understanding of language nuances. My gratitude extends to Wipf and Stock Publishers for their confidence in this project. Their dedication to advancing religious scholarship is commendable, and it is an honor to become a part of their esteemed cadre.

I extend my heartfelt gratitude to Elisabeth Rickard, Rebecca Abbott, and George Callihan at Wipf and Stock Publishers. Elisabeth, in particular, deserves a special shoutout for her academic prowess and meticulous attention to detail that significantly enhanced the quality of this manuscript. Her role as a copyeditor was instrumental in refining and elevating the content to meet the highest standards of scholarly excellence.

Like any meaningful journey, mine too was fraught with challenges. Each stumbling block, each hurdle, however, only served to enrich my understanding, deepening my appreciation for the intricate tapestry of theological discourse. As I navigated the landscapes of Old Testament theology, New Testament theology, historical theology, and systematic theology, I was driven by a singular aim: to establish natural theology as a distinct discipline. The task of learning ancient languages—classical Greek, classical Hebrew, classical Latin—though formidable, unveiled the wisdom of the church fathers and classical theologians in a way that would have otherwise remained obscured.

Emil Brunner's theology served as a lighthouse guiding me through the tumultuous seas of theological discourse. His steadfast commitment to uncovering the objective truth of God's revelation in his creation resonated deeply within me, influencing the course of this book.

As the concluding words of this narrative recede into the ether, I invite you to cast a final, reflective glance over the path we have traversed together. May the insights and revelations gleaned from our shared expedition enhance and invigorate your personal quest to understand the interconnected domains of theology, philosophy, and politics, as we collectively work towards a more equitable, sustainable world. The original title of this dissertation, submitted to Goethe University Frankfurt in 1995, was: "Die Bedeutung der religionsphilosophischen Methode und die Frage der natürlichen Theologie bei Emil Brunner."

Consider this scholarly work an affirmation of the enduring relevance of Brunner's theology, his resolute endeavor to reconcile faith and reason, and the consequential implications for current perspectives on religious-philosophical methods and natural theology. As you delve deeper into the complex web of Brunner's thoughts, may your intellectual journey be enlightening and enriching. May it inspire you to further contemplate the intricate intersections of theology, philosophy, and the contemporary social landscape, as we collectively endeavor to understand and navigate the vast and complex terrains of human knowledge and belief.

Yours in the quest for wisdom and understanding,
Baek, Dong In
September 15, 2023

PROLOGUE

SET BEFORE US IS the task of dissecting the distinctive theology of Emil Brunner, a theological fabric woven autonomously yet intricately entangled with the warp and weft of Karl Barth's dialectical theology. Crucial is this odyssey of intellectual exploration to fully grasp the theological trajectory of Brunner, and his wrestling with Barth's thunderous "No!" to natural theology—a refusal that resulted in their ideological divergence. This resonating "No!" cast long shadows over Brunner's standing among German-speaking theologians, subtly diminishing the allure and scrutiny of his work.

In the vein of Barth before the dawn of World War I, Brunner initially found himself ensnared between the poles of liberal theology and religious socialism. However, akin to Barth, Brunner too rejected any theology of mediation in due course. His magnum opus, *Mysticism and the Word*, was a rigorous critique of Friedrich Schleiermacher's theology, a work that caught even Barth off guard with its intensity.

The development of Brunner's Christology, a task he undertook prior to Barth, presented him with a formidable challenge: reconciling human articulation with theological principles. This led him to draw a demarcation between formal and substantive verbal ability. However, his choice of the term "point of departure" to signify this formal verbal ability stirred up a maelstrom of confusion, and is often seen as the catalyst for Barth's emphatic rejection.

The theological narrative of Brunner unfurls over three distinct phases: the journey of religious understanding up to World

War I, the theology of the Word until his parting of ways with Barth, and lastly, the concept of Truth as Encounter. This narrative underscores a theologian who painstakingly sculpted his unique theological perspective over time.

In the inaugural phase, Brunner perceived himself firmly embedded in the framework of consciousness theology, a school of thought that owes much to Schleiermacher. His dissertation, "The Symbolic in Religious Knowledge," is a quintessential testament to this phase. Guided by Schleiermacher's principles, Brunner endeavored to carve out an independent experiential value for religion.

During this period, Brunner was significantly swayed by the contemporary philosopher Henri Bergson. Bergson's theory of knowledge, known as the intuitive method of knowledge, held a particular appeal for Brunner. This method accentuates an immediate understanding that acknowledges both the individual and the whole, standing in stark contrast to the causal and atomistic approach. As Brunner articulates it, it's an "inner perception."

Brunner seamlessly integrated this religious intuition with John Calvin's "*testimonium spiritus sancti internum*," or the internal witness of the Holy Spirit. Essentially, the Transcendent or the Absolute, while distinct from humans, can be experienced via intuition or the "witness of the spirit."

Symbols assumed a vital role in Brunner's theological framework during this phase, as they provided a language for the ineffable. Brunner conceived that at the deepest stratum of human experience, one could unearth both the moral and religious, which could only be expressed symbolically. Two primary symbols that Brunner employed were the "supra-human personality" and the "spiritual supraworld."

Transitioning towards dialectical theology, Brunner renounced key tenets of his previous theological stance. He critically engaged with Bergson, whose work he had earlier admired. Ultimately, Brunner concluded that the revelation of God's will was paramount. This epiphany prompted a shift in Brunner's theology, supplanting the concept of intuition with that of faith.

PROLOGUE

Brunner incorporated the concept of the I-Thou relationship into dialectical theology, drawing from Martin Buber and Ferdinand Ebner. Yet, for Brunner, there was no initial discord between dialectical and dialogical theology. In his oeuvre *The Mediator*, he grappled with the ethos of the nineteenth century and advocated for a unique, historically specific revelation of Christ.

A significant schism between Brunner and Barth emerged over the question of human nature. Barth vehemently repudiated the notion of humans being naturally capable of speech, positing that such assumptions could inadvertently obstruct divine grace's redemptive work. Brunner sought to bridge this schism by conceiving the encounter between God and humans as an existential relationship. However, Barth dismissed this line of argument, setting the stage for their ultimate ideological parting.

Brunner's concurrence with Barth on God's absolute claim was always tenuous, as the point of mediation, or the "Anknüpfungspunkt," was a contentious issue from the outset. Over the course of time, Brunner found his theological bedrock in the dialogical model as opposed to the dialectical model.

The final phase of Brunner's theological evolution was devoted to his interpretation of modern natural theology. Consistent with his previous stance, Brunner renounced the intuitive method, mysticism, and ethics as pathways to the divine. His 1937 work *Man in Revolt* marked a pivotal shift in Brunner's theological thought. He proposed that sin is integral to understanding human existence, portraying the human condition as inherently conflicted and distanced from God.

Nevertheless, Brunner construed the fall into sin as a fundamental opposition arising from being made in the image of God. Humans are in perpetual rebellion against God, and this revolt is also the root cause of all earthly revolutions. Despite this, sin does not prevent humans from recognizing natural laws and facts; but when it comes to their innermost selves, and thus their position towards God, delusion due to sin is most pronounced.

Yet, Brunner also contended that there is an ongoing restoration of the imago Dei in individuals who open themselves to the gospel. God's word encounters them in connection and resistance. While Brunner and Barth shared a similar perspective on this, Brunner emphasized the similarity between God as a person and the human person, enabling humans to be addressed by God.

God's word, according to Brunner, materially shapes personhood and sets a new beginning. This confrontational address of God's word is strictly personalistic and atonalistic. As such, the traditional figure of Christianity, as historically interpreted, falls away. For Brunner, God met humanity in Jesus, in a real, historical encounter that is present and simultaneous for everyone, echoing Søren Kierkegaard's concept of contemporaneity.

However, Brunner still distinguished between formal and material imago Dei. Despite the perversion and obscuration caused by sin, the world still testifies to God's creation. Barth's view of creation, oriented towards Christ, appears more sharply defined than Brunner's perspective, which differentiates between a formal and material imago Dei.

The problem then arises: Brunner's doctrine of "the human in contradiction" does not align with his doctrine of general and existential revelation. Brunner's assertion that sin and true encounter coexist implies that there is no history of Adam. Yet, his image of the human remains that of a sinful being confronted with the revelation in Christ. In addition to this revelation, Brunner also acknowledges a general revelation, which contains the formal imago Dei. This duality led to Barth's protest.

The focus of this work is the development of Brunner's dogmatic approaches. The three stages of his theological development—liberal theology, theology under Barth's influence, and his independent standpoint—are described in depth. However, these stages are not absolute; elements from each stage intermingle and influence each other, creating a dynamic and evolving theological perspective. This is the labyrinthine landscape of Brunner's theology—a landscape shaped by intellectual struggle, ideological divergence, and continuous evolution, ultimately manifesting a unique theological voice that echoes through the annals of theological discourse.

INTRODUCTION

Problem and Method

THE TERMS DOGMATICS AND eristics, nature and grace must be considered paradoxical. In general, Lutheran doctrine emphasizes "that salvation is not achieved through human works but is based on God's free grace."[1] A problem arises from their modern ambiguity within the sciences. However, their usage within theological research is also far from uniform. For example, Yorick Spiegel states in his book on Schleiermacher:

> If nature were changed by sin, this would be something that does not belong in dogmatics. In contrast to social evils, natural evils should only be seen as punishment for sin to the extent that they affect the awareness of God.[2]

Dietrich Bonhoeffer also touches on this point:

> Because in the light of grace, everything human and natural sinks into the night of sin, one no longer dares to pay attention to the relative differences within the human and natural out of fear that grace may suffer loss.[3]

For Karl Barth, since the beginning of the twentieth century, grace has been important as the embodiment of Christian

1. See Otte, "Gnade V," 8:496ff.
2. See Spiegel, *Theologie der bürgerlichen Gesellschaft*, 182.
3. See Bonhoeffer, *Ethik*, 152–53; Bonhoeffer goes on to say that it is cheap to experience "grace without discipleship, grace without the cross, grace without the living incarnate Jesus Christ" (*Nachfolge*).

existence and is described as the "triumph of grace."[4] Therefore, Karl Barth speaks of the revealing God:

> God reveals Himself.[5] He reveals Himself through Himself. He reveals Himself. This God Himself is not just Himself, but also what He creates and accomplishes in people . . . It is God Himself, in indestructible unity, the same God who, according to the biblical understanding of revelation, is the revealing God and the event of revelation and its effect on people.[6]

Each commitment to one of these perspectives must face all other perspectives. Otherwise, one's own image of God is in danger of reflecting one's own religious search. If the event and effect of revelation are not God himself, our knowledge of God is at best a result of inferring from the existence of revelation to the revealing God. Therefore, in contrast to Barth's "ingenious one-sidedness," the other "task of theology" must be proclaimed:

> It is the task of our theological generation to return to the right theologia naturalis.[7]

To do this, the correspondence between divine and human word must be maintained. The fact that such a correspondence exists, that is, that we can talk about God, proclaim his word, is objectively because God has created us in his image, and subjectively, that this is revealed in Jesus Christ. The incarnation of God is the basis for understanding the truth and depth of the divine image in humanity, but the indestructibility of the divine image in humanity on a formal level is the objective possibility for divine revelation in his "Word." For "even the Church relies on being able to talk about God with people at all."[8]

---

4. See Otte, "Gnade V," 8:504.
5. See Barth, *Kirchliche Dogmatik*, 1/1–2.312.
6. Barth, *Kirchliche Dogmatik*, 1/1–2.315.
7. See Brunner, *Natur und Gnade*, 44: For Brunner, grace is a central concept that distinguishes religion and is essential to Christian-biblical knowledge of God.
8. Brunner, *Natur und Gnade*, 41.

INTRODUCTION

After this brief description, it should be clear how difficult but important the problem of the point of connection is. With Brunner, the focus is on the point of connection itself. Therefore, the solution to the problem is not initially to be found in faith but is a contemporary issue. Of course, this sharp antithesis cannot remain, and there is a certain approximation during the discussion.

The task of discussing the problem of the point of connection in confrontation with Brunner is limited in two ways. On the one hand, from the abundance of questions about nature and grace in their historical development, only those that Brunner has dealt with in his studies have been singled out. This limitation of the topic is justified for purely historical reasons considering the great inspiration that Brunner has provided for wide circles, including the author of this writing. Whether it is also systematically justified, or whether fundamental pieces of the problem are being overlooked, can only be shown by the investigation itself.

On the other hand, Brunner is only discussed to the extent that the confrontation with him leads to the presented topic. Therefore, the task is to present Brunner's theology in its development. It becomes clear that, despite all changes and precisely in them, Brunner's thinking has remained surprisingly unified. To do this, it is essential to look at the modern questions surrounding the concept of the point of connection, namely in theology in relation to the natural sciences and the modern worldview. Therefore, limiting the topic to the terms "nature and grace" in the narrower theological sense is just as impossible as restricting it to the occurrence of the terms "nature" and "natural." While Brunner's theology has already been presented, it still seems appropriate to me to reiterate Brunner's essential thoughts for the presented topic to prevent unjust "consequences."

FIRST PART

Brunner's Understanding of Religious Knowledge and Symbolism as the Origin of Religion in His Early Period (1914)

1.1. RELIGION: KNOWLEDGE OR EXPERIENCE?

Brunner's most important work from his early period is his dissertation on the epistemological topic "The Symbolic in Religious Knowledge."[1] In this work, which he dedicated to his "teacher and mentor"[2] L. Ragaz, he aims to develop a theory of religious knowledge by searching for criteria for the truth of religious statements in religious consciousness. He approaches the question of religious knowledge as a question about the truth of the religious, not about the truth of Christian faith.

Like Karl Barth or Adolf Schlatter, Swiss theologian Emil Brunner (1889–1966) emerged from parish ministry. Nevertheless, he provided important impulses for the entire Christian church: his view of the revelation of God and the resulting ecumenical and social behavior. Already socialized in the Christian faith, his

---

1. With his dissertation "Symbolic in Religious Knowledge: Contributions to a Theory of Religious Knowledge," he obtained his licentiate degree in 1913 (published as Brunner, *Symbolische in religiösen Erkenntnis*; see Krause and Müller, *Theologische Realenzyklopädie* [*TRE*], 7:236).

2. See Brunner, "Spiritual Autobiography," 4: "As a pupil and under Ragaz's auspices I wrote my first book, *Das Symbolische* (1913), at the age of 23."

FIRST PART

confirmer Hermann Kutter in Zurich opened his eyes to religious-philosophical problems and the concerns of the religious-social movement. Above all, the idea of God's claim on all life should be adopted by Brunner from Kutter and further defined. During his studies in Zurich and Berlin, he had other important theological teachers, including Adolf von Harnack, Julius Kaftan, and Leonhard Ragaz.

Brunner attempts to develop a theory of religious knowledge by using the concept of symbolism to construct an independent theory of religious knowledge. In this endeavor, he follows a modified version of Schleiermacher's theory of consciousness. Brunner aims to achieve a unique synthesis of Kant and Schleiermacher.[3] For him, Schleiermacher's fundamental thesis about the peculiarity and independence of religious consciousness from all other psychic phenomena is the "secure basis of all further developments."[4] Pure consciousness analysis is the foundation of all determinations. Therefore, religious knowledge is the latent knowledge of a transcendent reality contained within the moral norm consciousness.[5] Access to the world of faith is opened through the experience of the absolute and the superiority of nature and the experience of independent "spirituality."

On the other hand, there is also the danger of boundless subjectivism—and, ultimately, of illusion. This danger must be countered with Kant's demand for the rational justification of religious objects. However, Kant does not question the validity (i.e., the truth) of religion, but he sees it as dependent on practical reason, namely on the criterion of moral consciousness.

---

3. Brunner, "Spiritual Autobiography," 5ff.

4. Brunner, "Spiritual Autobiography," 3; see also the conclusion: "I hope that I have at least succeeded in giving a clear expression to the conviction that religion, religious life, can never be replaced by philosophical speculation. What is accessible to religious knowledge, that is her own possession, which she does not need to share with anyone else, a sanctuary that admits no one else" (Brunner, "Spiritual Autobiography," 132).

5. Brunner, "Spiritual Autobiography," 13, 49ff.

For Kant, the decisive interest of rationality, i.e., the normative validity of religion, is directed towards practical reason. He seeks and finds a substitute for the validity that scientific propositions possess in moral norms.[6]

Thus, Brunner does not accuse Kant of ignoring the question of the truth of religion,[7] but of seeking it outside of religious consciousness. Ultimately, Kant's view of religion is lifeless and pale, only a kind of appendix to ethics.[8] The objects of religious knowledge, God, eternal life, and freedom, appear as mere postulates of practical, i.e., moral reason. For Brunner, the answer to this question of truth lies in religious consciousness, as it contains elements that are "evident, i.e., immediate and valid."[9] Brunner is aware that this determination is based on the idealistic concept of knowledge, "according to which truth cannot be established by comparison with actuality, but only by qualities of consciousness, by the character of evidence."[10]

For him, this idealistic theory of knowledge is a premise that is not critically questioned. He relies primarily on the works of Sigwart, Windelband, and Rickert. This theory is particularly evident in the work of Henri Bergson, who has drawn a sharp distinction between the lifeless, static world as an intellectually conceptual object of knowledge and the intuitively recognizable unified, indivisible, animated world, as well as space and time, matter, and consciousness."[11] Only within this framework is the autonomy of religion preserved for Brunner.[12]

---

6. Brunner, "Spiritual Autobiography," 2–3.
7. Brunner, "Spiritual Autobiography," 3.
8. Brunner, "Spiritual Autobiography," 3.
9. Brunner, "Spiritual Autobiography," 5.
10. Brunner, "Spiritual Autobiography," 6.
11. See Bergson, *Einführung in die Metaphysik* (quoted as "Introduction"), 5.
12. Bergson, *Einführung in die Metaphysik*, 9–10. Here he returns to the idealistic use of the concept of religion: "We find ourselves once again on the ground of idealism, which alone provides space for the autonomy of religion." Regarding the idealistic assumptions, see also pages 42 and 47ff.

FIRST PART

In addition to this idealistic presupposition, a second one appears, also adopted from Bergson: his philosophy of intuition. Brunner adopts from it the criticism of epistemological intellectualism. Within the scope of our topic, we do not consider it necessary to delve further into Brunner's philosophical justifications for his religious epistemology. It remains to be noted here that he strives to demonstrate, based on Bergson's philosophy, the inevitability of the intuitive method of knowledge, which will eventually become a central part of his conception of religion.[13] Brunner sees the necessity of intuition in that some mental activities can only be explained by it.[14] Brunner believes that intuitively gained knowledge cannot be expressed, at least not in the same way as knowledge directed towards spatial things and relations.

> Therefore, intuition, immediate knowledge, as knowledge of the simply individual, peculiar, unique, is not expressible or at least not to the same extent as the knowledge of spatial things and relations.[15]

Brunner aims to arrive at a new concept of truth through the exploration of "deeper sources of knowledge" that convey an "immediate adequate knowledge" which is not rationally justified but experienced, and only through this process of experiencing can it become part of objective consciousness. He defines this as a "particular form of knowledge through inner perception, intuition."[16] This concept becomes the essential key term of the entire treatise as it reflects the philosophical premises on which the theory of religious knowledge is built.

---

13. Bergson, *Einführung in die Metaphysik*, 5ff.
14. See Volkelt, *Gefühlsgewissheit*, 43.
15. Brunner, *Symbolische*, 8.
16. Brunner, *Symbolische*, 129ff; 50n1: Brunner himself refers to Schleiermacher's expression "unity of feeling and intuition"; see Schleiermacher, Second Speech in *Über die Religion*, 22–23; "Über seine Glaubenslehre," §3. Brunner emphasizes, like Schleiermacher, the feeling of dependence in the religious experience. Brunner's conception of religion is closely related to Schleiermacher's.

1.2. THE INTUITION FOR RELIGIOUS KNOWLEDGE

The following aims to identify the motives that lead to the development of religious consciousness. The process of forming religious beliefs is followed and, from this, criteria for truth are elicited. The analysis of consciousness is the only way to carry out this process.[17]

Every theory of knowledge first asks: How does a person come to knowledge? The Aristotelian-Scholastic philosophy gave the answer to this question: "The material conveyed to us by the senses must be processed by the intellect to arrive at knowledge."[18] Thus, the actual tool for recognition is the intellect, and the senses are the medium of recognition; they provide the material to be recognized. According to Aristotle, the intellect has two aspects: a passive (*nous pathetikos*) and an active (*nous poietikos*). Knowledge of things arises when the passive intellect receives sensory perceptions, and the active intellect forms non-sensory concepts from the sensory material received. These concepts contain the true essence of things.[19]

The active intellect forms judgments by logically connecting concepts that correspond to sensory perceptions. The judgments thus formed express the true knowledge of an object or the knowledge of the relationship between several objects.[20] Brunner criticizes Scholasticism for "accepting untested views as immutable, axiomatic truths and building a worldview on such dogmas."[21]

Hegel further developed the Scholastic approach. He made the products of the intellect, the concepts, the basis for further knowledge acquisition. A comprehensive understanding of reality arises from the logical combination of concepts (speculation), which the intellect also performs. Thus, for Hegel, the intellect is the primary factor in knowledge acquisition.

---

17. Brunner, *Symbolische*, December 7, 1966.
18. Brunner, *Symbolische*, 1.
19. See Hirschberger, *Geschichte der Philosophie* 1:180–81.
20. Hirschberger, *Geschichte der Philosophie* 1:180-81.
21. Hirschberger, *Geschichte der Philosophie* 1:180-81.

FIRST PART

The intellectualism emanating from Aristotle attempts to recognize God intellectually, i.e., by applying logical laws, particularly the principle of causality. Aristotle presents God as self-contained, like logical laws, as an *ens a se immutabilis*. In contrast, Hegel believes that logic is not fixed and lawful but in a constant state of flux.[22] Accordingly, he proclaims a God of becoming, formally identical to this logic. With dialectical thinking, Hegel believes he can explain everything conceptually related, including the concept of "God." Hegel thus presents the concept of God dialectically: infinite, absolute being creates its opposite, i.e., finite, relative being, the world, from itself; it negates or spiritualizes this world simultaneously, while recognizing itself as spirit in its cancelled opposite. This self-awareness creates a consciousness of absolute being.[23]

The philosophy tasked with dialectically unfolding the concept of God is destined, according to Hegel, "to attain a recognition of the necessity of the content of the absolute notion, i.e., the notion of God."[24] Dialectical philosophy negates religion and its ideas of God by creating absolute knowledge of God. This absolute knowledge is no longer knowledge of the knowledge of God but God's knowledge of himself in humans.[25] In this way, a concept of God is formed that, because it moves and develops from itself and "eternally acts, creates, and enjoys itself as absolute spirit, the eternal and self-existent idea," serves as the starting point for religious knowledge in Hegel's religious intellectualism. Hegel no longer questions the origin of this self-existent idea, nor its conditioning by the intuitive act of the religious person, which is why he loses sight of the existential dimension of knowledge of God.[26]

---

22. See Lakebrink, *Hegels dialektische Ontologie*, 83–84, 87.

23. See Staudenmaier, *Darstellung und Kritik*, 845.

24. See Hegel, *Enzyklopädie der philosophischen Wissenschaften*, §527, 581.

25. See Küng, *On Being a Christian*, 253–54; see Kern, "Relationship between Knowledge and Love," 399, 413. Hans Küng criticizes Hegel following Walter Kern, but continues Hegel's thoughts on a "Dialectic of Love." Küng's "Dialectic of Love" corresponds roughly to Brunner's truth mediated dialogically, i.e., a "Truth as Encounter."

26. Hegel, *Enzyklopädie der philosophischen Wissenschaften*, §577, 598–99.

Emil Brunner disagrees with this view and presents his own understanding of the nature of religious knowledge.

> For Kant, the essential factors are the moral norms with their claim to absoluteness. Only the experience of their regularity can enable religious knowledge. For Kant, the decisive interest of reason, that is, the normative validity of religion, is directed towards practical reason. He seeks and finds a substitute for the validity that scientific propositions possess in moral norms.[27]

While Kant separates religion and science, Schleiermacher distinguishes between religion and morality.[28]

> In fact, he drew even sharper lines than Kant did, separating the view of God from the view of the world by not allowing the justification of religion to be based on the moral consciousness.[29]

According to Schleiermacher, the origin of religious knowledge lies in the consciousness of "absolute dependence of humans on a divine being." He refers to this consciousness as the truly pious feeling.[30] However, this feeling must already be present for a scientific investigation of religion and its object to be possible. The object of religion would be a specific manifestation of this feeling of absolute dependence on a divine being.[31] The position that occupies the "consciousness of absolute dependence on God" in Schleiermacher is taken up by Kant through the experience of the "claim to absoluteness of the norm." Schleiermacher goes beyond Kant because he seeks God within the human being and does not understand God, as Kant does, as an object of the sensually and intellectually perceptible external world. Schleiermacher applies the results of Kant's critique of knowledge to his philosophy of religion. As the first theologian, he did so appropriately.

27. Brunner, *Symbolische*, 5.
28. Schleiermacher, *Über die Religion*, 33.
29. See Stange, *Christentum und moderne Weltanschauung*, 42.
30. See Schleiermacher, *christliche Glaube*, 2:23.
31. Schleiermacher, *Über die Religion*, 43.

FIRST PART

What Kant accomplished in other areas of philosophy; Schleiermacher accomplished in the philosophy of religion. Kant is the father of critical philosophy, but in the philosophy of religion, he is still bound to pre-critical views. Schleiermacher is the critical philosopher of religion par excellence.[32]

Brunner sees epistemological approaches in both Kant and Schleiermacher that offer certain problems in each. Although Brunner constructs his view of religion on the third antinomy of Kant's cosmological ideas, and while Kant also bases his ethics on this proposition and both have a formal similarity in their conceptual structure, the relationship between Brunner and Kant remains an unresolved question in detail.[33] However, it can be said that Kant builds his ethics on the freedom of the intelligible self, which follows a moral law.[34]

> With the idea of freedom, the concept of autonomy is inseparably connected, and with this, the general principle of morality, which is as much the basis of all actions of rational beings as the law of nature is the basis of all determinations. And so categorical imperatives are possible because the idea of freedom makes me a member of an intelligible world.[35]

In contrast, Brunner takes this third antinomy as a starting point for his philosophy of religion, which deals with the subject's dependence on an authority that does not coincide with the self. Brunner sees the problem with Schleiermacher that he attributes a tendency towards illusionism to religion because it is essentially driven by pious sentiment.[36]

Brunner attempts to save religious knowledge from this weakness by positing the capacity for inner vision or "intuition"

32. Nygren, *Dogmatikens vetenskapliga grundläggning*, 69.
33. See Kant, *Kritik der reinen Vernunft*, 389, 448; see *Grundlegung zur Metaphysik* (*GMS*), 79–80.
34. See Kant, *Religion innerhalb der Grenzen*, 51; see Kant, *GMS*, 78–79.
35. Kant, *GMS*, 78–79.
36. Schleiermacher, *Über die Religion*, 6.

in all intellectual areas of human experience, a concept he draws upon from Bergson and from Kant. He refers to something that influences the feelings, thoughts, and consciousness of a person, and which, because it has such a comprehensive influence, enables access to transcendence, to God.[37] Especially for the self-consciousness, intuition has an excellent significance, as it unites the areas of knowledge and has a mystical dimension according to Bergson and Brunner.[38] The intuition attempts to gain metaphysical knowledge from all intellectual, logical, and conceptual aspects combined. Ultimately, as Karl Rahner observes, intuition as such leads every philosophy to a dead end in its metaphysical unfolding.[39]

Bergson's philosophy survives such a consequence because he philosophizes with the intellect, which he had previously brought into concepts as the enemy of philosophy.[40] Brunner strives to demonstrate that the religious world and access to its truth can only open to humans if they seriously explore their own intellectual personality:

> In the experience of independent spirituality, the access to the world of faith is opened to me, but that experience is not blown to me, but it becomes real to me only through participation of my moral will.[41]

However, this endeavor must also consider the awareness of the moral norms that determine humans. Nevertheless, according to Brunner, the religious world is open to every intuitively acquired vision obtained through this approach.[42] Brunner believes that the intuition has the precise task of leading subject and object

37. Schleiermacher, *Über die Religion*, 78, 130.
38. Bergson, *Einführung in die Metaphysik*, 5ff.
39. See Otte, *Lernen*, 36: In reference to Karl Rahner, Otte states: "According to the empirical-critical didactics, the question methodologically used to synthesize the different conditions seems to be sufficiently clarified, as it is observable everywhere in the empire."
40. See Salakka, *Person und Offenbarung*, 38.
41. Brunner, *Symbolische*, 131.
42. Brunner, *Symbolische*, 131.

FIRST PART

together,[43] and the gap experienced between the religious world and the person determined by moral norms closes when the free intellectual personality becomes aware of itself as a subject and understands its connection with universal spiritual being from this consciousness. Brunner sees the subject and object of religious intuition in a "trans-subjective unity from within":

> If we want to look inwardly at our spirituality, to bring it to consciousness through intuition, then the Other is given to us just as immediately as its qualitative nature: the connection with something comprehensive, the participation in something that goes beyond us; and this objectivity is not something new that is added to what we had before: rather, a moral consciousness comes about only where this objective feature is present, where I know myself to be determined in a peculiar way by something that I am not, or as part of a spiritual being. With this, we have what we were looking for: a trans-subjective connection from within, i.e., one obtained from the nature of the spiritual.[44]

1.3. RELIGIOUS KNOWLEDGE IN ADDITION TO INTUITION

When asking how to understand the phenomenon of religion, Brunner believes that religion attempts to explain the motives behind the emergence of religious consciousness. Furthermore, every religion is based on fundamental religious knowledge that cannot be abandoned and is passed down throughout history:[45] "Religion has its foundation in the self-evaluation of humans."[46]

Therefore, the intuitive self-reflection in which humans experience themselves in their spirituality can be referred to as a religious primordial act. According to Brunner, this process

---

43. Brunner, *Symbolische*, 49.
44. Brunner, *Symbolische*, 49.
45. Brunner, *Symbolische*, 12–13.
46. Brunner, *Symbolische*, 13.

represents an immediate relationship with God that can only be achieved through self-reflection. Without the fundamental experience of God, religion is not possible. As there are many diverse forms of this fundamental experience, each recognition of God has its specific content.[47] Great religious personalities are of particular importance for this religious recognition, which is conveyed from outside, as "in such religious heroes, that supernatural spiritual life and at the same time the religious consciousness open up to us ordinary people the religious world much more powerfully, purely, and clearly than our own experiences."[48]

Therefore, the spiritual realm inherently possesses a trans-subjective connection "from within."[49] The trans-subjective and transcendent reality is thus related to the experience of the Absolute, the Supernatural. Intuitive experience grasps reality, and in doing so, the subject experiences itself as determined by these values.[50] As religious knowledge can be exceptionally great in some individuals who are particularly gifted intuitively, many people could gain possession of this knowledge through the personal charisma or corresponding teachings of the individuals.

Brunner emphasizes in this context that most major religions can be traced back to the unique work and teachings of a single personality. This guarantees that intuition, i.e., the path to religious knowledge, is not associated with an individualistic, privatizing understanding of religion.[51] Young Brunner calmly accepts the accusation of a "subjective-mystical religious theory" that arises from this understanding, as from his perspective, he can also criticize Kant's decidedly anti-mystical way of thinking:

---

47. Brunner, *Symbolische*, 14.

48. Brunner, *Symbolische*, 15; see Josef Hasenfuß, "Heros," in Höfer and Rahner, *Lexikon für Theologie*, 5:268–69; see also Hofmann, "Heroismus," in Höfer and Rahner, *Lexikon für Theologie*, 5:267; Meyer, *Konversations-Lexikon*, "Heros," 9:230: "In the modern sense, Heros means a person who surpasses human measure in a particular field."

49. Brunner, *Symbolische*, 48–49.

50. Brunner, *Symbolische*, 17, 49.

51. Brunner, *Symbolische*, 15.

> If I had not myself lived for years on the border of the mystical country—and sometimes even in its midst—I would neither have had to write nor could have written this book. It is the struggle against a near—very near to us all—enemy ... Those who have believed in the compatibility of both from youth on, having read and loved the Bible in the light of idealistic philosophy and mysticism, and having read and loved the mystics and idealists in the light of the Bible, know how bitter it is to admit that this synthesis so suggested to us by history is an illusion and perhaps the most dangerous of all temptations.[52]

On the one hand, Brunner describes intuition and the resulting mysticism as "the heart of religion"; on the other hand, there exists an objective element of revelation that influences the mystical experience of the individual and corrects it, if necessary.[53]

According to Brunner, intuitive knowledge correlates with the subjective witness of the Spirit, the "testimonium spiritus sancti internum."[54] He defines intuition as brought about by the Spirit itself. In this context, the corresponding concept to the "unio mystica cum Christo," i.e., the becoming one with Christ—who is encountered in the external word of Scripture and in preaching—is the adoption of objective revelation.

The formulas "testimonium spiritus sancti internum" and "unio mystica cum Christo," which Brunner mentions, show his closeness to Calvin. Calvin, namely, traces the cognition of God through Scripture and faith essentially back to a "testimonium spiritus sancti that is intus and arcantus."[55]

The content of religious experience is the experience of the Absolute,[56] which is objective, independent of the subject's needs, and valid in and of itself. Thus, religious knowledge is caused by

---

52. Brunner, *Symbolische*, 6, 15, 51; see also Brunner, *Mystik und Wort*, vi.
53. Brunner, *Symbolische*, 15.
54. Brunner, *Symbolische*.
55. Brunner, *Symbolische*. See Calvin, *Institutio Christianae Religionis*, 3:68/70, 446; 4:191; 7, 4–5; 1. 7, 4–5; 11.12, 7; 3.11, 10.
56. Brunner, *Symbolische*, 16.

two factors: (a) intuition or the witness of the Spirit, and (b) objective revelation or *verbum externum*.

However, it should be noted that the content of religious intuition shows that subject and object do not become identical in religious experience.[57] Nevertheless, intuition is the actual basis for it.[58] The religious heroes' concepts of God are objective realities, but they only arise through the workings of particularly strong, empathetic intuition.[59] With the symbol "the supra-world," Brunner wants to express the transcendence of this universal spiritual being, through which the subject is determined in religious experience.[60]

For Brunner, both the mediation and appropriation of objective revelation are bound to intuition, without which intuition would remain dead and ineffective. Pre-existing religious knowledge can lose its significance due to this intuition and be replaced by completely new knowledge. Existing religious traditions can therefore only claim conditional validity. As the final norm of religious knowledge, the focus is not on the given, such as dogma, but on the spirit, because what the spirit is "cannot be taught by thinking or imagination, but only by that inner perception which we call intuition."[61] In summary, Brunner's presentation of the fundamental religious content also points to intuition as the first path to religious knowledge.

1.4. THE CONCEPT OF RELIGIOUS KNOWLEDGE: "SPIRITUAL SUPRA-WORLD" AND "SUPRA-HUMAN PERSONALITY"

The intuition is directed towards the spiritual areas within humans and from there it creates an access to transcendence and shapes a

---

57. Brunner, *Symbolische*, 60.
58. Volkelt, *Gefühlsgewissheit*, 43.
59. Brunner, *Symbolische*, 87.
60. Brunner, *Symbolische*, 47.
61. Brunner, *Symbolische*, 59.

concept of God. Generally, humans have a spiritual certainty that they differ in their mode of existence from natural things and are superior to them.[62] This is best illustrated by the example of morality, which appears as a consciousness of norms within the consciousness itself (categorical imperative) and carries the character of absolute validity and independence from everything natural. This characterizes the so-called spiritual values.[63] Every person can absolutely adhere to a norm.[64] This absoluteness can only have its origin in a "peculiar spiritual being," a "spiritual supra-world, not in nature or in humans themselves."[65] The consciousness is intuitively "led out by the nature of its object, the personal spirit, to the recognition of a universal spiritual being."[66]

This consciousness of man about himself presents itself both as unity and as diversity. The aspect of unity includes the consciousness of the spiritual personality, which experiences itself as free. On the other hand, the experience of dependence on the universal spiritual being can be understood as an expression of diversity.[67]

The supernatural spiritual being experienced in unity and diversity, i.e., in internal intuitive perception, "constitutes the content of religious knowledge, the knowledge of God."[68] However, the experience of freedom of the spiritual personality can only be fully understood by becoming aware of this person's limitations. This limit differs significantly in nature from the compulsion of the law of causality. Without the experience of freedom, man feels bound to the norm.[69] Behind every norm, there is something simple, which is why every norm makes the same claim of

---

62. Brunner, *Symbolische*, 13.
63. Brunner, *Symbolische*, 13.
64. Brunner, *Symbolische*, 44.
65. Brunner, *Symbolische*, 49.
66. Brunner, *Symbolische*, 13.
67. Brunner, *Symbolische*, 13.
68. Brunner, *Symbolische*, 13.
69. Brunner, *Symbolische*, 13.

absoluteness on man.[70] A moral awareness of norms arises, which carries the thought of the "comprehensive spiritual being" with it. Brunner summarizes this awareness under the term "supra-world" "and equates it with God. God is included as a "moral spirit in the spiritual."[71] As such, he is infinite.[72]

The content of knowledge of God is based on religious consciousness, and in two ways: firstly, as consciousness of a spiritual realm that transcends the world of human spirit. Secondly, it also involves a spiritual personality that is equally absolute and stands above human personality. These two factors, supra-human personality and infinite moral spirit, are the components of religious consciousness that are "evident in a similar way, immediately and validly as the propositions of logic and ethics":

> If we do not want to fall into boundless subjectivism, we cannot avoid Kant's rational justification. If we do not want to violate the living, distinctive, peculiar religion, we must also try to understand its "knowledge," i.e., statements of being, from within it and not from external perspectives, and attempt to distinguish true from false. Both postulates are fulfilled if we can find within religious consciousness itself components that are "evident" in a similar way, i.e., immediate, inseparable, and valid, as the propositions of logic and ethics.[73]

They determine the essence of religion.[74] Brunner distinguishes here between the essence and the empirical appearance of religion.[75] The religious experience is determined by absolute values, which are objective, independent of the subject's needs, and therefore inherently meaningful.[76] These religious values enable the subject, who is grasped by an intuitive experience, to have

70. Brunner, *Symbolische*, 53.
71. Brunner, *Symbolische*, 49ff., 52ff., 73.
72. Brunner, *Symbolische*, 65, 132.
73. Brunner, *Symbolische*, 65, 132.
74. Brunner, *Symbolische*, 12–13.
75. Brunner, *Symbolische*, 11.
76. Brunner, *Symbolische*, 16.

a vision of the universal spirit.[77] Brunner repeatedly emphasizes the awe of the religious experiencing subject before the holy being outside of himself and describes this feeling as perceptible in the cult.[78] However, for Brunner, the distinction between the essence of religion and its empirical appearance remains essential.[79] Spiritual life dominates over purely natural life, and the clarity of spiritual concepts determines how the essence of religion can still be expressed in the empirical appearance. This also applies to all living religion, because in it, the transcendence of God dominates over his consciousness immanence.

"The overwhelming importance of the objectivity factor in immediate experience"[80] thus influences this fundamental attitude in an essential point: the trans-subjective, the non-self of religious consciousness, thus gains the weight that gives transcendence experience its significance.[81]

This intense experience ultimately stands in contrast to humans' consciousness of an identity with God. While a separation between God and man is thus maintained, the possibility of a relationship remains, even if it initially seems to hinder intuitive recognition. The immanence of God in consciousness proves to be epistemologically motivated: in fact, God-centeredness and knowledge of God can only be gained through a kind of existential connection, that is, they can only be experienced through God's dwelling in the spiritual being of man.

For this, man must be able to grasp in the divine something that is akin to his own nature, only then can he recognize the divine as a spiritual being in which he shares through this coincidence. In this ability to recognize, the immanence of God is once again

---

77. Brunner, *Symbolische*, 17, 49.

78. Brunner, *Symbolische*: "The fundamental experience in all religion is the experience of the holy"; see Windelband, *Sacred in Preludes*, who recognized the feeling of the holy in religious experience as essential very early on.

79. Brunner, *Symbolische*, 14.

80. Brunner, *Symbolische*, 51.

81. Brunner, *Symbolische*, 48–49.

revealed. In this way, man can experience the reality of God in his own existence, experience it, intuitively see it, and thus recognize it.

Through contemplation, we experience the divinity.[82]

For Brunner, the fundamental contents of religious knowledge arise from religious consciousness. Despite the danger that they may be viewed as an illusion or projection of the religiously conscious individual, he emphasizes that "the transcendence of the divine does not need to be abandoned... which would amount to human deification."[83]

He demonstrates the transcendence of the divine in religious knowledge by describing the symbolic nature of every religious understanding as essential. These symbols are "the supra-world" and "personality." The symbol of the supra-world determines the consciousness of the subject through the religious experience. In it, the subject experiences the transcendence of this universal spiritual being.[84]

Personality is the symbol that expresses the formal similarity of the subject with the object. This similarity is based on the experience of the religious experience, that is, on the experience of the connection between ego and God. It is clear that "personality is a symbol for God's immanence."[85]

---

82. Brunner, *Symbolische*, 130.

83. Brunner, *Symbolische*, 19.

84. Brunner, *Symbolische*, 47.

85. Brunner, *Symbolische*, 58, 60: "The religious consciousness is such that it requires the symbol of personality to express the objectively given within it"; "But the symbol of personality, as a correlate of the momentary consciousness, that is, of our connection with God, is an expression of immanence."

1.5. THE SYMBOLIC UNDERSTANDING OF GOD THROUGH RELIGIOUS KNOWLEDGE

1.5.1. The Sign and Expression Function of Symbols

Brunner is looking for a method to better illustrate the principle than with the term "symbol." The intuitively acquired knowledge should emerge from the mystical veil of wordlessness. The theory of symbols is helpful to him for this purpose.[86]

> In the symbolic way of thinking, one always deals with a double-object consciousness, with two ideas that stand in a peculiar relationship of representation to one another.[87]

Brunner understands symbol consciousness to mean consciousness of this representation.[88] According to Brunner, a symbol must fulfill two conditions to be meaningful and scientific.[89] Brunner distinguishes between the sign function and the expression function of the symbol, depending on where the emphasis is placed.[90] The characteristic of the sign function is that the symbol points to something that it is not itself.[91] If the symbol is to represent an expression function, there is a certain similarity or affinity between the symbol and what it represents. Brunner differentiates between affinity and similarity.[92]

---

86. Brunner, *Symbolische*, 20.

87. Brunner, *Symbolische*, 21.

88. Brunner, *Symbolische*, 21: "Symbol is that in which another is recognized."

89. Brunner, *Symbolische*, 22: "If the symbol is to achieve its purpose, i.e., if it is to be a meaningful and scientifically usable sign, it must clearly point to the relevant content and exert a compulsion on the objective consciousness to go beyond the immediately given in a certain direction."

90. Brunner, *Symbolische*, 20, 26.

91. Brunner, *Symbolische*, 22.

92. Brunner, *Symbolische*, 22.

The buzzing of a bear is "similar" to the sound of a diesel engine. Common characteristics can be identified through logical analysis.[93]

This is not possible with affinity, as it is considered intuitive. Brunner uses the expression "piercing smell" as an example. When analyzing these two words—smell and piercing—no similarity can be found. However, experience teaches us that there are olfactory perceptions that are like piercing. This similarity is intuitive and not the result of analysis:

> The similarity that we find in genuine symbols is in fact a "deeper," "darker, more mysterious" one than the . . . so to speak, logical one.[94]

By illustrating both similarity and affinity, the symbol not only points to what is symbolized but also expresses and represents it.[95]

> Since it does not fully meet this requirement (analogy instead of equality), it also takes on the function of a sign, i.e., it points to something else.[96]

Thus, Brunner's understanding of symbols allows for a connection to Thomas Aquinas's concept of analogy. Thomas refers to the middle ground between word equality and meaning equality as analogy.[97] For example, according to Thomas, God is called wise in a different sense than humans because God surpasses all human abilities. However, this is not in mere word equality (such as "cross" can mean both a mere sign and human suffering) since there is an internal similarity between God's wisdom and that of humans.[98]

---

93. Brunner, *Symbolische*, 30.
94. Brunner, *Symbolische*, 30.
95. Brunner, *Symbolische*, 26.
96. Brunner, *Symbolische*, 27.
97. See Aquinas, *Summa theologia*, 1q. 13, a. 5 (1:274).
98. Aquinas, *Summa theologia*, 1q. 13, a. 5 (1:274).

In Thomas's theology, there are ideas that parallel those of Brunner. These ideas have their origins in the Platonic thinking of the philosophy of Aristotle and Augustine. For example, Thomas assigns an analogical meaning to the name of God.[99] Plato already explains this concept of analogy, also called proportionality analogy. Aristotle develops the concept of relational equality, such as 6:3=4:2. He derives it from geometry (intellectualism). In contrast, Thomas goes back to Plato's typical idea of participation.[100]

According to Brunner's view, every religious insight is symbolic. The pre-understanding of the name of God and thus God himself is like this. The symbol gains its expressive power through the inner participation of the symbol object in the essence of what is symbolized.[101]

According to Brunner, partial agreement between the symbol and what it symbolizes cannot yet be called similarity.[102] The connection can be described as a correspondence between the realms of consciousness, which can only be grasped through a total intuition and not a priori analysis.[103] Since the correspondence between the realms of consciousness enables the coexistence of all psychic and spiritual phenomena, and "primarily appears to us in the form of symbolism, it gains immeasurable significance for spiritual life."[104]

For Brunner, participation in the Transcendent means "a relationship similar to momentary existence, as belonging to the spiritual rather than the spatial order." Recognizing that the origin of all moral and religious life lies in the depths of the soul, Brunner considers the role of the symbol in this area to be of the utmost importance.[105] "In these 'depths' we also find those central activities of the soul, the moral and religious, and it is known that this is

---

99. Aquinas, *Summa theologia*, 1q. 13, a. 5 (1:274).
100. Hirschberger, *Geschichte der Philosophie*, 1:485.
101. Hirschberger, *Geschichte der Philosophie*, 8-9.
102. Brunner, *Symbolische*, 29.
103. Brunner, *Symbolische*, 30.
104. Brunner, *Symbolische*, 32.
105. Brunner, *Symbolische*, 57.

the true home of the symbol."[106] The symbol can rightfully be considered the "language of the ineffable," as it gains more significance "the deeper we penetrate into the depths of consciousness."[107] There is an inner connection between the symbol and religious knowledge, which will be examined more closely in the following.

1.5.2. The Symbolization of Religious Knowledge

The symbolization of religious knowledge refers to the internal experience that provides access to both the expressive and indicative function of the symbol. The content of religious knowledge is the awareness of God as a "suprahuman personality" and a "spiritual transcendent realm." For Brunner, these two concepts are already expressions of a symbol consciousness. The symbol of "suprahuman personality" is meant to illustrate the personality of God that goes beyond all human measures.[108]

The "spiritual supra-world" stands for the objectivity of God. Brunner refers to the transcendent, i.e., God, as "world" since there is an inner relationship between the objectivity of the world experience and the religious experience.[109] An objective relationship is constitutive to a moral experience. The religious consciousness belongs to the realm of the spiritual-moral, but it is not the moral itself. Rather, it is referred to as "the way in which man becomes intuitively aware of this spiritual life." Through this awareness, the transcendent spiritual being is perceived. "The source of moral behavior can be seen as God. Thus, moral behavior points to God."[110] Brunner adopts the claim of unconditional norms from the realm of morality.[111] They constitute a world of moral virtues

106. Brunner, *Symbolische*, 38.
107. Brunner, *Symbolische*, 38. Brunner adopts from Bergson the role of intuition in the realm of self-consciousness (see Bergson, *Einführung in die Metaphysik*, 5ff.).
108. Brunner, *Symbolische*, 61.
109. Brunner, *Symbolische*, 59.
110. Brunner, *Symbolische*, 132.
111. Brunner, *Symbolische*, 67.

that appear in an ideal and unimaginable way to humans and point to the world of God.

For humans, the spiritual world comes, so to speak, from outside, objectively towards them,[112] in contrast to the personality symbol for God, which comes from within. They both have the same object in view as a whole but emphasize different aspects.[113]

The ambivalent or transcending character of the symbol gives it a key function in its ambiguity. It allows the transition from the finite to the infinite, from the conditional to the unconditional. It creates a connection between God and humans. The experience of the superhuman personality is for Brunner more inward and immanent than is the case with the spiritual world. From this, it follows that God, the object of religious knowledge, can only be grasped and described in symbols.

However, for Brunner, only the two main symbols presented so far, "spiritual world" and "superhuman personality," are primarily illustrative. Consequently, the linkage of religious basic elements with objects of the human and worldly sphere is not yet complete in the illustrative symbols. With these objects,

> the religious consciousness . . . merges into the idea of God, the religious object, the sensually present God.[114]

This presence of God as an object does not only mean existence and being, but also the activity of God.[115] As a result, the divine personality, which relates to the personal being of man and is immanent in it, appears as present in a pictorial way.

However, Brunner does not deny the significance of the individual person, as he believes that as a metaphysical spiritual being, the individual preserves an epistemological significance that must be considered. But the individual can only comprehend God as their origin and their goal as a spiritual personality.[116] As soon as a

---

112. Brunner, *Symbolische*, 49.
113. Brunner, *Symbolische*, 59.
114. Brunner, *Symbolische*, 98.
115. Brunner, *Symbolische*, 100.
116. See Jalkanen, *1909-1924*, 30-33 (summarized in German in *Person*

person is aware of themselves as a person, they also know of their unity as a spirit-body or soul-body unity.[117] Therefore, without the predicate of the personality of God, religious consciousness is not possible at all.[118]

In the symbol of heaven, the world beyond, which actually expresses the transcendence of the divine, takes on concrete form.[119] According to Brunner, there is a direct relationship between this symbol of heaven and the original Christian concept of the kingdom of God,[120] as "the character of the kingdom is closely linked with transcendence."[121] Both represent a fixed reality that is not created by humans, but which humans can only participate in.[122] Brunner's theological roots regarding the interpretation of the concept of "the kingdom of God" can be found in the Ritschl circle, which limited one-sided individualism with his teaching by linking God's rule to a moral community.[123]

However, Ritschl does not see his teaching on the kingdom of God as contradicting the individual concept of personality, because

> it is precisely in the realm of the Kingdom of God that man (according to Ritschl) succeeds in freeing himself from the shackles of nature, which are the worst hindrance to the development of his free personality, and in finding a field of activity for his moral abilities and powers.[124]

For Brunner, the kingdom of the supra-individual spirit means a retreat of the individual, the personality.

---

und *Offenbarung*, 57).
117. Brunner, *Symbolische*, 113.
118. Brunner, *Symbolische*, 113.
119. Brunner, *Symbolische*, 121.
120. Brunner, *Symbolische*, 121.
121. Brunner, *Symbolische*, 121.
122. Brunner, *Symbolische*, 121.
123. See Ritschl, *positive Entwicklung der Lehre*, 17.
124. Jalkanen, *1909-1924*, 69.

The correlation concept to heaven in Brunner is Father, which is only an expression of his conception of God. No specific father is meant, but the essence of the concept contains a spiritual content and no concrete object.[125] According to Brunner, this concept symbolizes the entire reality of God, both his transcendence and immanence, as well as his objectivity and subjectivity, his demanding claim, and his caring encouragement.[126] The connection of the two secondary symbols, human and kingdom of heaven, lies in Brunner's idea of the "dwelling" of God, "in heaven" or the "rule" of God in his kingdom.[127] But does the experience of transcendence really appear as a correlate to that epistemological justification of the spiritual connection between God and man, or is it simply neglected due to the interest in the immanence of the divine?

1.6. SUMMARY: RELIGIOUS KNOWLEDGE AND SYMBOL

Emil Brunner's dissertation "The Symbolic in Religious Knowledge" addresses the question of the truth of religious statements and attempts to develop a theory of religious knowledge by identifying criteria for truth within religious consciousness. He follows Schleiermacher's theory of consciousness, which posits that religious consciousness is independent of other psychic phenomena and constitutes the foundation of everything else. Brunner seeks to synthesize Schleiermacher's theory with Kant's demand for a rational foundation of religious objects, but accuses Kant of seeking truth outside of religious consciousness, making his view of religion lifeless and colorless. Instead, Brunner sees the answer to the question of truth in religious consciousness itself, relying on the idealistic concept of knowledge and the intuition philosophy of Henri Bergson to critique epistemological intellectualism. Brunner believes that intuitive knowledge, gained through inner

---

125. Brunner, *Symbolische*, 123.
126. Brunner, *Symbolische*, 123.
127. Brunner, *Symbolische*, 123.

vision or intuition, cannot be expressed rationally, and seeks to arrive at a new concept of truth conveyed through immediate and adequate knowledge that is experienced rather than rationally justified. Brunner criticizes the Aristotelian-Scholastic philosophy's approach to knowledge, which relies on untested views as irrefutable truths and builds a worldview on them.

There are various approaches and philosophies regarding religious knowledge. The Aristotelian-Scholastic philosophy regards the mind as the tool of cognition, while Hegel's philosophy takes the concept as the basis for acquiring knowledge. Kant regards moral norms as essential factors for religious knowledge, and Schleiermacher emphasizes the significance of the consciousness of ultimate dependence on a divine being. Brunner seeks deeper sources of knowledge through intuition and experiences immediate, unrepeatable knowledge. He regards intuition as an essential tool of cognition and an integral part of objective consciousness. The concept of intuition becomes the key concept of his entire treatise and reflects the philosophical premises on which his theory of religious knowledge is built.

Brunner's philosophy of religion critiques the epistemological approaches of Kant and Schleiermacher. He believes that religious knowledge can be saved from illusionism by assuming the ability of inner vision or intuition in all areas of human intellect. This allows access to transcendence and closes the gap between the religious world and human determined by moral norms by bringing together the subject and object of religious intuition in a trans-subjective unity from within. Brunner sees religion as based on fundamental, irreducible insights that are passed down through history and have their foundation in the self-evaluation of the human being. The intuitive self-reflection in which the person experiences oneself in their spirituality can be seen as the religious primordial act. Brunner emphasizes the importance of the personal influence and teaching of religious personalities, as this guarantees that the path to religious knowledge is not associated with an individualistic, privatizing understanding of religion. He stresses the importance of intuition as the primary path to religious knowledge, directing itself towards the spiritual aspects of human beings and creating access to transcendence from there. Brunner sees the human being as having a spiritual certainty that distinguishes their existence from that of natural things and makes them superior, particularly in the realm of morality.

Brunner's philosophy of religion emphasizes the importance of intuition as the primary path to religious knowledge, providing access to transcendence through spiritual aspects of human beings. The content of religious knowledge is constituted by the supernatural spiritual being experienced as both unity and diversity. Religious consciousness includes the immediate validity of the consciousness of themselves as free and of the supernatural realm as absoluteness, which is a prerequisite for religious knowledge. Brunner also uses the theory of symbols to better illustrate intuitively obtained knowledge. The symbol must indicate something that it is not itself, fulfilling the sign function, and requires a certain similarity or affinity between symbol and symbolized to fulfill the expression function. The symbol can represent the symbolized through similarity or affinity but does not fully meet the demand for equality, also taking on the function of the sign by indicating something else.

Brunner argues that religious knowledge is necessarily symbolic, and the relationship between symbol and symbolized is not simply one of similarity. Instead, he sees the relationship as a relatedness that belongs to the spiritual order and allows access to the consciousness of God as a superhuman personality and a spiritual transcendent. Symbols are particularly important in the moral and religious areas, where they express the unspeakable and gain meaning as we penetrate deeper into the soul's life. The symbols of the spiritual transcendent and the superhuman personality create a connection between God and humans, and God can only be grasped and described through symbols. The predicate of the personality of God is essential to religious consciousness. Brunner links the symbol of heaven with the concept of the kingdom of God and sees a correlation between them. However, the experience of transcendence can be neglected due to a focus on the immanence of the divine. Brunner believes that religious knowledge cannot be verified by criteria from other areas, such as ethics, and that the truth of religious knowledge must be found within religious consciousness. Symbolic knowledge is indirect, but it allows access to the material objects of God, and the knowledge of God presupposes a relationship of similarity and analogy between God and humans.

In summary, Emil Brunner's theory of religious knowledge emphasizes the importance of intuition and symbolism in accessing the transcendent realm and understanding God. He criticizes the epistemological approaches of Kant and Schleiermacher and seeks to develop an independent theory of religious knowledge that is based on the consciousness of morality and dependence. Brunner sees religious knowledge as symbolic and emphasizes the importance of participation in the transcendent as a related relationship that belongs to the spiritual order. Different concepts of God lead to different forms of religion, and religious heroes can obtain knowledge through deep intuitive achievements. Brunner's theory of religious knowledge is based on the latent knowledge of the consciousness of morality of a transcendent world, which he derives from within. However, if there are contradictions in his statements about the consciousness of morality and dependence, his theory of religious knowledge loses its foundation.

SECOND PART

Brunner's Theological Development after 1921

2.1. TRANSFORMATION TO DIALECTICAL THEOLOGY

2.1.1 Brunner's Transition to Dialectics

For Brunner, the five-year interruption of his literary work after the publication of his dissertation resulted in a creative break. During this time, as a pastor of the small mountain community of Obstalden, he engaged in practical pastoral work.

In 1919, at the Aarau Student Conference, where he informed himself on the topic "Thinking and Experiencing,"[1] he heard a lecture by Heinrich Barth on "The Knowledge of God" that impressed him greatly. Barth's philosophical conception provided important impulses for Brunner's thinking, which should not be underestimated: they concerned both the understanding of the philosophical task in the narrower sense as well as critical aspects that Brunner addressed in his confrontation with the various forms of subjectivism. Above all, Brunner found in Barth a philosophical self-understanding that placed philosophy and theology, thought and faith, in a fascinating relationship. Barth, who saw the intellectual foundations of his philosophy "in Plato, in the Christian world of thought, in rationalism, in Kant and Fichte, and in the Marburg School," "defined the field of philosophy as

---

1. *Vorträge*, 5–34.

the realm of the Word, which was in the beginning, and through which everything was created."² It becomes clear that the synthesis that had been formed five years earlier from the mystical-subjective experience (Schleiermacher) and the ethical objectivism (Kant), and whose unifying bond was emotional intuition, is now breaking apart.³ Although Brunner does not yet give up his concept of intuition, he formulates it more purposefully: the individual subject has lost its significance. In doing so, he once again sets himself apart from intellectualism, which he had already met with sharp criticism earlier.⁴

In 1920, Brunner published "The Misery of Theology," a short programmatic writing that represents a process of intellectual ferment and challenges old truths that were once considered axioms.⁵ The writing "The Misery of Theology" reflects Brunner's theological upheaval prior to the announcement of the dialectical program. He proposes four points there that, in his opinion, should form the methodological cornerstones of modern theology and that need to be critically explored: the rejection of causality, the intuitive introduction method, and a certain rejection of psychologism and historicism. The questions posed in this theological reorientation clearly connect to the antithesis formulated by Karl Barth in his struggle against the "modern-traditional task assignment" during his critical early period. From this contextual connection, it can be

2. See H. Barth, "Gotteserkenntnis," 225.

3. See Spiegel, *Theologie der bürgerlichen Gesellschaft*, 58. Spiegel mentioned him as follows: "At the same time, Schleiermacher is interpreted in terms of an opposition that did not yet exist for him, namely the opposition between an ethical and a naturalistic concept of religion (as already in the 19th century, but also in Emil Brunner), and thus the opposition between personal and a-personal, i.e., societal relationship."

4. See Brunner, "*Römerbrief* von Karl Barth."

5. In 1919, Karl Barth (not to be confused with Heinrich Barth) critically engaged with psychologism in the Tombach lecture. Shortly after the publication of Barth's *Romans*, Brunner welcomed Barth's focus on the over-psychological and absolute nature of faith. This made Barth objective. The objective-divine spirit thus comes into its own differently than subjective-human consciousness. (see Barth et al., *Anfänge der dialektischen Theologie*, 185–86). Brunner may have engaged with Barth's position from a Christological perspective.

concluded that Brunner received inspiration for the new orientation of his thinking precisely from this direction.[6]

Only in 1921 did Brunner publish another major treatise, namely *Experience, Knowledge, and Faith*, with which he demonstratively aligned himself with the theological movement emanating from Barth and Gogarten. Both Barth and Gogarten are mentioned in his preface. Brunner admits that he could have said some things better and perhaps didn't need to say some things at all if he had received Karl Barth's second *Romans* and Gogarten's *Religious Decision* earlier.[7] He could only make use of some of the important insights presented in those works with some slight modification. Here too, Brunner fundamentally denies intellectualistic thinking. However, in *Experience, Knowledge, and Faith*, unlike in his first work, he differentiates between a perfectly reasonable and a misguided activity of the intellect. This would have to lead to a fundamental revision of his relationship to Bergson's philosophy of intuition. The following questions press on Brunner: "whether this entire [Bergson's] evaluation of the intellect is justified, whether Bergson's epistemological solution is satisfying . . . and whether other possibilities should be sought and in what direction."[8]

Brunner articulates a response to his new understanding, namely, "that within the understanding two opposing tendencies assert themselves, of which Bergson has only grasped the one leading downwards, without doing justice to the other upward tending, although it is precisely this tendency that owes the convincing power of his arguments."[9] The main principle of this tendency, the élan vital, is pure interiority, immediate contact with the source of life, a return to one's own non-rational origin.

6. See Brunner, "Elend der Theologie."

7. In his postdoctoral thesis *Erlebnis, Erkenntnis und Glaube* [*Experience, Knowledge, and Faith*], Brunner calls for a break with modern neo-Protestant theology with its historical relativism, its psychological inwardness, and its intra-worldly kingdom of God practice (iv).

8. Brunner, *Erlebnis, Erkenntnis und Glaube*, 63.

9. Brunner, *Erlebnis, Erkenntnis und Glaube*, 64.

"The élan vital, more convincingly than any other philosophical concept, unites the two moments that time seeks: It is pure interiority, immediate contact with the source of life; and it is the creative energy of life itself."[10] Brunner observed "under the influence of Bergson's anti-intellectualism in cognitive understanding, above all the lack of originality and immediacy."[11] He also notes the dissolution of the vital wholeness through analytical dissection as well as its artificial reconstitution in a self-created conceptual system. Like the researcher who eliminates the beauty of a flower by dissecting it, the intellect is like Ahasverus, the "eternal Jew," who never rests in his pursuit of his goal. He is an eternal skeptic, a heathen who does not give faith any room. The intellect leaves people cold; it robs the most sensitive and delicate fragrance from the beauty of life.[12]

But isn't Bergson's sharp conceptual analysis also "a bravura performance of the intellect? Doesn't the intellectual, by being judged here, regain its validity?" When the intellect is stuck before an inexplicable problem, when the question of life arises, for Brunner the principle of reason becomes increasingly inadequate compared to the creative, spiritual life.[13] "The intellect, as the ability to comprehend meaning, is nevertheless not only analyzing and explaining externally, but also grasping meaning, showing a Logos behind all reality."[14] "Thus, the intellect is both a tool for analyzing reality and a principle that transcends reality in terms of meaning."[15] The only means of defense against intellectualism is to make God's cause itself valid,[16] where God's cause is the Word of God that was in the beginning, the Logos.

10. Brunner, *Erlebnis, Erkenntnis und Glaube*, 21.20.59; see Brunner, *Symbolische*, 129ff., as well as the Aarau lecture "Thinking and Experiencing" (1919), some of which is included in *Erlebnis, Erkenntnis und Glaube*, 65ff.

11. Brunner, *Erlebnis, Erkenntnis und Glaube*, 60–62.

12. Brunner, *Erlebnis, Erkenntnis und Glaube*, 8, 10, 13, 25–26.

13. Brunner, *Erlebnis, Erkenntnis und Glaube*, 27.

14. Brunner, *Erlebnis, Erkenntnis und Glaube*, 69–70.

15. Brunner, *Erlebnis, Erkenntnis und Glaube*, 71.

16. Brunner, *Erlebnis, Erkenntnis und Glaube*, 74–75.

God is logos, the word that was in the beginning. Therefore, one can only experience him as one experiences spirit, meaning, truth, not as an object of perception, as mysticism would have it.[17]

One can only perceive it by listening to God's thoughts within oneself, metaphorically speaking. In this living thinking, which "harbors that relationship to the beyond and therefore the consciousness of its own inadequacy," the will of God is revealed to human beings. "This is the common testimony of the correctly understood Gospel and the correctly understood Plato."[18]

Here, there is continuity, i.e., an unbroken connection between the postulated infinity and the eternity of the soul. Brunner observes that this is not mystical contemplation, but rather "the simple thoroughness of thinking, its self-reflection on its own actions, the critique of reason by itself."[19]

It is clear here how Brunner adopts the thoughts of Karl Barth's dialectical theology.[20] Brunner testifies to "great respect for the significant intellectual work of Karl Barth," points to his 1919 review of Barth's work *The Epistle to the Romans*, and attributes great importance to Barth's development of the "objectivity of faith" for the further development of theology.[21]

---

17. Brunner, *Erlebnis, Erkenntnis und Glaube*, 74–75.
18. Brunner, *Erlebnis, Erkenntnis und Glaube*, 75–76; see P. Natrop (about himself) in Schmitt, *deutsche Philosophie der Gegenwart*, 165ff., 176; in Brunner, *Mystik und Wort*, this is clearly documented. However, Brunner does not hold fast to the antithesis of word and self or world understanding; see *Mystik und Wort*, 99, for Brunner, reflection (of faith) is the thoughts of God. Also, "this immanence of the logos, this innermost being-connectedness of the soul with its life-ground in its own depth, this mysticism of thinking is the prerequisite for that insight into the ultimate ground."
19. Brunner, *Erlebnis, Erkenntnis und Glaube*, 83.
20. See Volk, "Christologie bei Karl Barth," 3:613–15.
21. Brunner, *Erlebnis, Erkenntnis und Glaube*, 55n1.

2.1.2. Brunner's Concept of Faith Based on the Analogy between God and Humans: Theology of the Word

2.1.2.1. The Relationship between Faith and Psychology

In the following, we will discuss religious and theological psychologism, a new spiritual movement that Brunner, influenced by Barth, attacks as opposed to intellectualism. "Religion, faith, and theology follow the basic principles of psychologism, so God as an object of human experience and feeling should be empirically demonstrable."[22] Here, everything non-material, i.e., spiritual, is subsumed under the term "psychological events" and thus becomes the object of psychology. However, it becomes clear that "psychologism is unable to understand the spirit as such and to express specific conceptions of spiritual life."[23]

Therefore, Brunner speaks emphatically in this context of the "objectivity of faith." Ultimately, this is about the fundamental contrast between transcendence and immanence, which appears in the reality of the spirit. According to Brunner, psychologism misunderstands the transcendent character of the spiritual. It is a "monism of interiority, false immanence, ignores the spirit in the spiritual."[24]

> Psychologism is "the struggle for the otherness of faith, for the otherness in relation to humans and nature, for the cessation of more or less and mere relative certainty of experience" and the struggle that "we today are obliged to undertake against the romantic-pragmatic falsification of faith and the spirit."[25]

---

22. Brunner, *Erlebnis, Erkenntnis und Glaube*, 17, 41 ff., 58: Brunner "naturalizes" God by objectifying him. Even the spirit, understood as a fact, is a thing and not a spirit. Spirit and psychic factuality are, as it were, naturally different.

23. Brunner, *Erlebnis, Erkenntnis und Glaube*, 22–23n2, 331.

24. Brunner, *Erlebnis, Erkenntnis und Glaube*, 58–59, 100.

25. Brunner, *Erlebnis, Erkenntnis und Glaube*, 58–59.

According to Brunner, Schleiermacher was able to complete the religious feeling as the place of God-experience and with good conscience granted religion and theology independence from other sciences, such as philosophy.[26] Brunner's criticism of Schleiermacher did not begin in his book with the revealing subtitle *The Contradiction between Modern Religious Views and Christian Faith, Illustrated in the Theology of Schleiermacher*. After Brunner's lecture on Schleiermacher, Thurneysen wrote to his father:

> I was very pleased with the brave and fresh word. It was a sharp attack on modern theology, embodied in Schleiermacher, and a brave confession of the theology of the Reformers. The main emphasis was on the Reformers, with whose faith it was important to engage seriously. It seemed that the listeners, especially the younger ones, were following his words with tension.[27]

This polemical turn against Schleiermacher is already hinted at in Brunner's habilitation thesis[28] and reaches its peak in the programmatic "Epilogue for Theologians," which follows his inaugural lecture "The Limits of Humanity."[29] Brunner's critical questions to Schleiermacher, whether God is still the comprehensive Transcendent and Immanent if he only has one empirically verifiable possibility, namely, the pious feeling to reach humans, must be considered. Despite a critical distance from Brunner's dialectical critique of Schleiermacher, Thielicke questions whether Christian beliefs might not be weakened and impoverished by being reduced to "a sort of neutral location in the consciousness of pious feeling."[30]

26. Brunner, *Erlebnis, Erkenntnis und Glaube*, 19.
27. Barth and Thurneysen, *Briefwechsel*, 2:201.
28. Barth and Thurneysen, *Briefwechsel*, 2:4, 13, 16, 21ff., 33, 38.
29. See Brunner, *Grenzen der Humanität*; also published in *Anfänge der dialektischen Theologie*, 1:259–60, 272ff.
30. See Thielicke, *Introduction*, 34; see also *Introduction*, 33; Yorick Spiegel points out Brunner's sharp criticism; see *Theologie der bürgerlichen Gesellschaft*, 9: "Since the criticism of the cultural Protestantism that he defined by dialectical theology, the problem has remained undecided as to how a theology that replaces the Word with mysticism and knows God only from the feeling of

The assumption of an analogy between the spiritual and the material, between God and the world or humans, which formed the basis for a symbolic understanding of religious realities in Brunner's early writings, appears completely abandoned here.[31] "Here Barth's immediate God-human dialectic becomes apparent."[32] Barth's method brought to Brunner's consciousness the transcendence of faith as a theological fundamental category.[33]

But how should humans behave in the face of their radical distance from God to meet God? Here, Brunner refers to the self-forgetful hearing of God: the spelling out of the word of God. In accordance with Barth, he now calls it faith, not intuition.[34]

Thus, in his theologically grounded judgment on the problem of religious subjectivism, such as intellectualism or psychologism, Brunner follows the justification doctrine of Luther in consistent application. Where the anthropological question is carried out in this way, there exists work righteousness: Luther's theology is characterized by three negations—the intellectual-speculative, the mystical-inner, and the work-based-autonomous ladder to heaven—all of which are directed against a primal sin, namely, human self-assertion before and against God. Thus, Brunner is really polemicizing against a fundamental evil in human behavior toward God.[35]

---

absolute dependence can be reconciled with such intense social and political activity as that of Schleiermacher. Although Karl Barth has tried to defend Schleiermacher against Brunner's charge of a purely aesthetic religiosity."

31. Brunner, *Christliche Lehre von Gott*, 38.

32. Volk, "Christologie bei Karl Barth," 3:613–15.

33. See Brunner, "*Römerbrief* von Karl Barth," and in *Anfänge der dialektischen Theologie* 1:85: Brunner remarks on Barth's commentary on Romans: He counts it "among the highest merits of Barth that he dared and was able!—to bring to light again this timeless, over-psychological, absolute essence of faith, and that he manfully resisted all temptations to psychologism, which are so great for every modern person."

34. Brunner, *Christliche Lehre von Schöpfung*, 57, 75.

35. Brunner, *Christliche Lehre von Schöpfung*, 36; also see Nygren, *Eros und Agape*, 551ff.

The fundamental evil, the fall of theology and at the same time the pivot point at which the entire contrast between biblical-Christian faith and all general religion and piety is presented, lies in the assertion of a continuity of human existence with the divine. The depth of this contrast is later the occasion for Brunner to work on the understanding of evil, since taking evil seriously as sin and guilt implies the awareness of the shattered continuity, i.e., the separation of God and the world; this is the irreparable rift, the unbridgeable gap.[36] Here, together with dialectical theology, Brunner emphasizes the consistent contrast between God and the world.

2.1.2.2. The Relationship of Faith to History

Under historicism, Brunner understands that thinking that is convinced that it can explain the origin and purpose of history by describing history itself.[37] Within history, Brunner finds nothing that draws attention to its meaning and origin beyond itself.[38] He sees no approach within the historical realm for a possible mediation between God and humans, thus he has abolished all the popular natural bridges to God at his time.[39] In the tradition of Franz Overbeck, he does not oppose the separation of faith and history, that "Christianity began to reject history for itself and experienced it only against its own, originally expressed will," and it is not difficult to document Overbeck's influence in the formulation:[40]

> What the Christianity has done and experienced, reveals with unsurpassed penetration its relationship to history. It does not itself offer any prospect that it would be willing to defend itself based on historical knowledge. To place Christianity under the concept of history, to admit that it has become historical, means to admit that

---

36. See Brunner, *Mediator*, 97, 106–7, 259, 350.
37. Brunner, *Erlebnis, Erkenntnis und Glaube*, 102.
38. Brunner, *Erlebnis, Erkenntnis und Glaube*, 108–9.
39. Brunner, *Erlebnis, Erkenntnis und Glaube*, 108–9.
40. See Brunner, *Erlebnis, Erkenntnis und Glaube*, 107n1, 111n1; see also Overbeck, *Christentum und Kultur*, 79.

Christianity is of this world and has lived in it, like all life, only to express itself. Subject to the category of development, it also falls under the general scheme of historical contemplation of things . . . Transferred to the realm of historical consideration, Christianity is hopelessly subject to the concept of finitude or even decadence.

In the spiritual event of faith, Brunner speaks precisely about the breakthrough from another dimension into the realm of empirical reality, namely the breakthrough of the spirit of God into the world of givenness.[41] He concludes from this that one cannot take both God and history seriously.[42] In the Word of Revelation, he speaks of the eternal truth, which is not bound by time and is therefore the same yesterday, today, and forever. God has always revealed himself as who he is! Therefore, in this sense, truth is not something within history, but history is something within truth. Following Kierkegaard, Brunner sees simultaneity as the actual category of the word.[43]

"In the word, distance is abolished, immediacy and presence are formed, and truth is present." Brunner emphasizes emphatically that this objectivity of faith is superfluous through the trust of humans in God. Brunner distances himself from his intellectual forefathers, Schleiermacher and Ritschl:

> Schleiermacher began this doubtful business (confusing faith with trust) in his doctrine of faith, Ritschl promoted it, and modern theology has almost gone bankrupt on it; then everything depends on whether man can

---

41. Brunner, *Erlebnis, Erkenntnis und Glaube*, 108–9.
42. Brunner, *Erlebnis, Erkenntnis und Glaube*, 109.
43. Brunner, *Erlebnis, Erkenntnis und Glaube*, 109–10n1; see also Brunner, *Mensch im Widerspruch*, 220–21. Here the connection to the philosophy of language, which has long been hidden in conception and diction, becomes apparent. Already in the preface, Brunner sees man centrally from his "responsibility." Brunner owes his full understanding to the study of Luther: and the "acquaintance with Ebner, Gogarten and Buber" (see *Mensch im Widerspruch*, ch. 8).

bring himself to trust God, or not, trust then becomes his achievement.[44]

Although Brunner defended the understanding of symbols in his early days, it no longer corresponds to the earlier concept of symbols, as he now rejects the immanence of God in humans and the world, and thus denies the prerequisites of the expressive function of symbols; as a result, he degrades the symbol to a mere sign. In contrast to the symbolic significance of profane symbols, the deep dimension of the religious symbol is illuminated there.[45]

The extent to which Brunner turns away from analogical thinking and opposes the dialectic that divides God and the world or humanity is also evident in his understanding of faith, as "non-being as a mirror in which the divine countenance is reflected, membrane on which the divine word resounds purely, without any disturbing background noise, the utterly humble and reverential attitude that desires nothing but to be told by God, the unrestricted acceptance of what God speaks, what he is and will be for us."

According to Brunner, faith "is simply the repetition of what the divine truth declares"[46] and "nothing other than being directed towards God alone."[47] Therefore,

> ultimately, nothing else can be said about faith than that it is the understanding of God, the empty form that is nothing in itself but a vessel for this content and thus only expressible through its substance. Faith is purer the less can be said of it, the emptier it is in itself. Faith is pure objectivity.[48]

Doesn't Brunner's understanding of faith correspond to the foundation of Feuerbach's criticism of religion? However,

---

44. Brunner, *Erlebnis, Erkenntnis und Glaube*, 89–90: The identification of faith and trust leads, according to Brunner, to a moralistically flattened interpretation of the God-human relationship.
45. Brunner, *Erlebnis, Erkenntnis und Glaube*, 89–90.
46. Brunner, *Erlebnis, Erkenntnis und Glaube*, 93–94.
47. Brunner, *Erlebnis, Erkenntnis und Glaube*, 88.
48. Brunner, *Erlebnis, Erkenntnis und Glaube*, 89.

in contrast to Feuerbach's criticism, Brunner draws attention to the symbolic content of any religious knowledge and thus to the analogical relationship between Creator and creature. Now faith is entirely perceptible through its "objectivity, through the objective counterpoint of the Word that encompasses all words." Therefore, faith can only be named by its substance, which Brunner refers to as "pure objectivity." With this definition, he attempts to give the most appropriate expression to his antithesis against rationalistic religion, by no longer emphasizing negativity and criticism, but rather positive essence. "Pure objectivity expresses here an immediate relationship to divine truth, the complete devotion to it, and the humble acceptance of this truth." Thus, faith is "nothing other than the objective immersion of the divine sense, the becoming-for-me of the Logos, the recognition of grace."[49]

According to Brunner, the basis of this understanding of God does not lie in an irreconcilable dialectic between God and humanity, but rather in the "analogy of our relationship with our fellow human beings, in the I-Thou relationship."[50]

In his philosophy of I-Thou, Brunner primarily sheds light on the path towards a new understanding of the anthropological problem, whose urgency had become apparent to him starting from the question of humanity as the recipient of revelation. According to Brunner, "what we recognize from the Thou, what is for us from it, is meaning, attitude, meaning-determined limitation of our existence, in which we are included again as wanted and thought along. The Thou is nothing other for us than what we recognize from it."[51]

Therefore, we are already a real indication of God in our existence as primal meaning, final limitation, and determination willing and thinking person. The realization that personal being, contrary to the relationship-less and thus objectively relatable

---

49. Brunner, *Erlebnis, Erkenntnis und Glaube*, 91, 93, 96, 98, 124; see also his reference to the "categorical imperative of objectivity" (see K. Barth, "Wort Gottes als Aufgabe," in *Anfänge der dialektischen Theologie* 1:217).

50. Brunner, *Theology of Crisis*, 119–20.

51. Brunner, *Theology of Crisis*, 120.

being related to the objective world, is "existing being in the fundamental encounter of I and Thou."[52] To put it bluntly: the self acquires its being from the other and emerges through it. "I become through the Thou... All real life is encounter." The enduring merit of the Ich-Du philosophy is to have noticed and categorized the personal being, which is fundamentally distinct from the being of the world and things.[53]

Therefore, according to Brunner, faith in God and knowledge of God are not realized by ignoring everything human, but by looking at the true nature of interpersonal relationships.[54] It is remarkable that Brunner pursues dialogical thoughts in his transition to dialectical theology, but without acknowledging the tension that exists between them. Later, he turns entirely to dialogic thought and prepares his critique of Karl Barth's position from this perspective.

Brunner no longer assigns any significance to religious feeling for the revelation of God. For Brunner, both psychological mediations based on inner experience and feeling, as well as historical mediation based on individual historical events, fail. In this sense, for Brunner, it is

---

52. See Buber, *Ich und Du*, 18; also see Ebner, *Wort und geistigen Realitäten*, vol. 1. The image of man in theology culminates not in human abilities, but in a relationship. "The relationship with God, not reason, is the apex of the pyramid, the highest point in the hierarchy, as which man is built, and as which man is intelligible. Reason is only the organ of the relationship with God, as the soul is the organ of reason, and the material body is the organ of the soul. The peak of man, considered purely from man's perspective, is the self. But the self is what it is and what it should be, through the divine Thou" (see *Ich und Du*, 93). The imago Dei doctrine seeks to express this idea.

53. See Volkelt, *Gefühlsgewissheit*, 14ff., on Ebner's and Buber's philosophy of I and Thou. Ebner's new wisdom emerged from their respective engagement and further development of Kierkegaard's existential dialectic.

54. The foundations of Brunner's categorically grounded presentation of theological anthropology, which he presented in his book *Man in Revolt*, were laid by Ebner and Buber, as well as later by Griesebach and Gogarten. Their development of personality influenced Brunner's anthropological questions, as seen in his essays on "Gesetz und Offenbarung [Law and Revelation]," his lecture on Christian psychology, and his four studies on the personal being of God and man (1930).

principally completely indifferent to faith when, under which circumstances of time, in what historical context Christ lived, what preceded him and conditioned him. Faith is not historically oriented but oriented towards content.[55]

Besides the lack of transcendental capacity of history, Brunner presents another argument against the historical consideration of Jesus Christ. In faith, it is not about

> Christ being a son of David according to the flesh, but about him being vigorously proven to be a son of God according to the spirit, that he was sent by God, that he came from heaven to earth, that he brings and represents the "Word from Beyond."[56]

Therefore, Brunner disregards the temporal separation that exists between the present and the past existence of Jesus. Thus, he perceives Jesus as an immediate and simultaneous, but not as a historical person.[57] Only because he is a divine person, a divine "you," he is freed from the transience of time and history, and is present for us in faith at all times.

2.1.3. The Theological Position of Emil Brunner during This Period

Reasons for this change in Brunner's thinking can be partly seen in expressions in *Experience, Knowledge and Faith*. Brunner would

---

55. Brunner, *Theology of Crisis*, 104: "the biblical-reformational faith has nothing to do with the historical Christ or with becoming salvation . . . . The reformational faith deals, to put it briefly, with absolute greatness, and it can do so because it is not bound by the schema of nature and relativism: cause and effect but is under the category from which all absolutes arise. Reformational faith clings to the Word. Verbum Solum habemus. Not as a historical force, not as the beginning of a historical series, but as the Word of God to us, Jesus is the Christ of faith" (see also Brunner, *Mystik und Wort*, 220). "Thus the Jesus Christ of faith is no more the historical Jesus than the idea of the Christ" (Brunner, *Theology of Crisis*, 226.).

56. Brunner, *Erlebnis, Erkenntnis und Glaube*, 106, 122–23 (only in the 2nd ed.); also, *Mystik und Wort*, 220.

57. Brunner, *Erlebnis, Erkenntnis und Glaube*, 104.

never have been able to write his latest book "without the long-standing personal influence of a prophetic man," namely Hermann Kutter; equally influential for him were Christoph Blumhardt and Leonhard Ragaz—together, three leading theologians of religious socialism in Switzerland. In Kutter's theonomic theology, there is a common basis with the dialectical theology of Barth and Brunner.[58] Brunner's turn to dialectical theology seems to be in direct correlation with the change in the zeitgeist and religious sentiment during and after the First World War. His reaction to the spiritual-religious questions of the time already points to his later thoughts on the objectivity of God, the pure objectivity of faith, the dialectic between God and man, and the eternal divinity of Jesus Christ. For Brunner, the transcending of all provisional truth towards the ultimate interpretation unit of God is an expression of an objective fact.[59]

In the work *Experience, Knowledge and Faith*, in addition to all dialectical aspects, the idea of a genuine dialectical analogy between God and man can also be recognized.[60] Brunner repeatedly refers to this idea as well as to the analogical formulation of the "central truth in Pascal," stating:

> You would not seek me if you had not already found me, which Jesus expressed so simply in the parable of the lost son, that he was first with the father, at home, before he was lost.[61]

The internal prerequisite of the later Imago doctrine already benefits from its first conceptual form here. This idea is not

---

58. See Brunner, "*Römerbrief* von Karl Barth," 78–86 (Brunner fundamentally assessed the first edition of Barth's *Romans* positively): "The knowledge of the otherworldly Kingdom of God movement that emerges in Jesus from the hidden and reveals its goal in him: Immanuel"; see also Brunner, "Kirche und sozialen Forderungen [Church and Social Demands]"; see K. Barth *Römerbrief*, 439. Furthermore, Karl Barth's "second Romans" and Gogarten's "Religious Decision" helped Brunner to his new theological orientation.

59. Brunner, *Erlebnis, Erkenntnis und Glaube*, 46, 76, 95.

60. See Gestrich, *Neuzeitliches Denken und Spaltung* [*Modern Thought and the Division*], 33.

61. Brunner, *Erlebnis, Erkenntnis und Glaube*, 92n1.

abandoned by Brunner in his further works but is asserted and strengthened despite the protest of Barth and Thurneysen. Barth expresses his displeasure with Brunner's insistence on a human point of connection of revelation in the magazine *Zwischen den Zeiten*, which was founded in 1922 by him, Thurneysen, Gogarten and G. Merz.[62] The correspondence between Karl Barth and Thurneysen also raises the question of whether Brunner should be included in the inner circle of dialectical theology:

> "I would do it myself despite all concerns, because I find that the common presuppositions are broad enough, and even small peculiar doctrines that we do not approve of would not impair the whole." Barth considered: "I agree with a cautious use of Brunner..."[63]

Barth himself gave rise to this with his understanding of the first version of the *Epistle to the Romans*. There is still plenty of talk about immediacy, immediate unity with God, and the divine in man, and Brunner accentuates this aspect of Barth's thought. The reference was still on the level of the original understanding of God, on "that part of our soul that has not become attached to the temporal-finite but has remained an untouched divine reserve for the voice of God."[64] A certain skepticism towards Brunner's views is also reflected in the further exchange of ideas between Barth and Thurneysen.[65]

---

62. See in *Zwischen den Zeiten* [*Between Times*] 8 (1924) note 58.

63. Barth and Thurneysen, *Briefwechsel*, 2:145; see also 141.

64. Brunner, *Romerbrief*, in: *Anfänge der dialektischen Theologie* 1:81, 84; see also Jalkanen, *1909–1924*, 95 (as cited in Salakka, *Person und Offenbarung*, 58n25): Jalkanen writes that Barth did not yet have a sense against psychologism in his first lecture on Romans. This resulted in an extremely critical, almost Barthian view of Barth by Brunner.

65. Barth and Thurneysen, *Briefwechsel*, 2:293, 297, 320, 322, 699–703; especially better judgments, 357, 404.

SECOND PART

2.2. BRUNNER'S THEOLOGICAL ARGUMENTS BETWEEN GENERAL AND SPECIAL REVELATION (1927)

2.2.1. Assumption of Thought

Brunner's life's work is guided and shaped by two main intentions: the revelation of Jesus and humanity. These two themes are not disconnected loci in Brunner's thinking but are so closely intertwined that it is impossible to understand his understanding of revelation without his understanding of humanity, and vice versa.

Now we will examine how these themes encounter each other in theology. In the person of Jesus, divine transcendence and human existence come together. The question of humanity as the recipient of revelation, and the problem of the historicity of revelation as well as the existential reality of faith is a task that dialectical theology inevitably faces. Brunner, Gogarten, Bultmann, and ultimately Barth all sought answers to this question, albeit in different ways.[66]

In his period of dialectical theology between 1922 and 1928, Brunner took a sharp and decisive stance on this issue. His writings from that time are filled with the enthusiasm of the new awakening and full of dynamism and creativity, stemming from the separation from the traditional. They are at the same time an inexhaustible expression of his urge to bring newly recognized things to attention in constantly new ways and to help them break through.[67]

Ultimately, for him, the "anthropological" problem consists in the relationship between the divine and human subject. Before God, there is no calling for humans to act on their own. Rather, faith lives from the knowledge that it does not carry the basis and

---

66. See Barth's critical retrospective on the earlier study of dialectical theology in *Menschlichkeit Gottes* [*Humanity of God*] (1956).

67. See especially *Grenzen der Humanität* (1922), *Mystik und Wort* (1924), *Philosophie und Offenbarung* [*Philosophy and Revelation*] (1925), "Reformation and Romanticism" (1925), *Mittler* [*Mediator*] (1927), "Wrath of God and the Reconciliation through Christ" (1927), *Religionsphilosophie protestantischer Theologie* [*Philosophy of Religion*] (1928), etc.

justification for its knowledge within itself. However, the human being, as much as he or she is the object of sovereign divine grace, is a person and not a fact. But how can the unity of these opposites be found without depriving faith of its objective or subjective content? How is this possible without losing sight of the grace or act of faith, which is an anthropological problem? Brunner first points to the distinction between general and special revelation. He attempts to further justify his anthropological rethinking thesis that the theological currents mentioned above can do without God by pointing to the blurring of the distinction between general and special revelation in modern theology.[68]

2.2.2. The Possibility of Knowledge of God through Revelation in Nature

Brunner's break with the theology of the nineteenth and early twentieth centuries, that is, Schleiermacher's, Ritschl's, and Adolf von Harnack's, takes place in the writing *The Mediator*, a *Reflection on the Christ Faith*. According to Brunner's understanding, the title alone represents a correction of previous mystical-romantic, idealistic-speculative, and historically liberal theology. It also signifies a deliberate return to the "long-known and always repented," to the understanding of Christ "in ancient church doctrine and the Reformation."[69] His theological efforts are aimed at understanding the connection and opposition between God and humanity, at that encounter event that he describes as the "word-event,"[70] namely the relationship between "natural world knowledge and divine revelation mediation."[71]

---

68. See Brunner, *Mittler*, ix–x. In his Christology *Mediator*, Brunner emphasizes the Christian revelation as standing above all other general revelations. At the same time, he rejects the Jesus theology of the nineteenth and twentieth centuries.

69. Brunner, *Mittler*, v.

70. Brunner, *Mittler*, 178–79, 353.

71. See Pannenberg, *Basic Questions in Theology* [English version], 27: "Even before Barth, a 'Christology from above' was undertaken in modern

SECOND PART

For Brunner, general revelation, or more precisely "revelation as something general," means the

> emergence of an eternity ground of all phenomena that has always existed in consciousness, the realization of something that has always been true, the awareness of a divine presence that could have always been perceived.[72]

For Brunner, human, and world as something that has always existed is sufficient material for divine revelation. Therefore, here, revelation is human knowledge of God in and through nature.[73] Brunner distinguishes between two basic forms of appeal to revelation: (1) Folk religions refer to the manifold revelations with a massive character,[74] where the revelations are experienced as diverse manifestations of the divine-personal beyond world in this natural-historical world.[75] (2) The understanding of revelation is evident, among other things, in mysticism, religious speculation, religious philosophy, and the "religion of the educated." Here, revelation is the realization of the divine as it has always been there and can be perceived: as something general.

As Brunner recognizes divine truth in both tracks,[76] Christian faith belongs to neither the first nor the second group. However, both basic forms differ significantly from the specifically Christian understanding of revelation. Although philosophical, mystical, and general religious knowledge of God is full of deep, inherently untrue elements—a perversion of the truth—it is "not simply non-truth but rather partial truth, half-truth."[77] Therefore, the broken dialectical relationship between it and Christian faith can never be

---

theology, in the book 'The Mediator.' Brunner was the first among the 'Dialectical Theology' group to present such a Christological design."

72. Pannenberg, *Basic Questions in Theology*, 4.

73. See Denzinger and Schonmetzer, *Enchiridion Symbolorum* (hereafter D-S), 3026: This understanding of revelation is entirely consistent with that of the First Vatican Council on natural revelation.

74. Brunner, *Mittler* [*Mediator*], 3.

75. Brunner, *Mittler* [*Mediator*], 3.

76. Brunner, *Mittler* [*Mediator*], 6, 13.

77. Brunner, *Mittler* [*Mediator*], 6, 13.

one of supplementation, such as a basic revelation on which the revelation of salvation is based. Neither *Lex naturae*, the natural order, nor natural knowledge, natural theology, can be the foundation for the revelation of Christ, otherwise "the Christ fact would be emptied, and the image of the natural man distorted." Rather, Christian faith includes general revelation and general religion "as distorted truth in itself as its own precondition!"[78]

But what is the "precondition"? The material precondition of the reconciliation-revelation is here the revelation of creation and the situation of humanity determined by it. The general revelation is now placed within the comprehensive framework of a theology of creation and thus also theologically secured from its origin. Jesus Christ, the incarnation of God in time, is revelation and Logos.

> There is only one Logos. This Logos is only recognizable in Christ. But this Logos is the principle of all recognition and, above all, the truth kernel of all religion.[79]

The individual historical fact is not valued as a revelation event in general revelation. It is only based on the apparently general law behind all historical facts. The living religion and Christian faith are connected by the reference to a real revelation event in its historical particularity, contradicting the Fichte-word: "the latter only makes one knowledgeable."[80]

For Brunner, the essential contrast is thereby reduced to the difference between the fundamental immediacy and repeatability of the general religion or general revelation and the Christian faith in the unique revelation in the mediator Jesus Christ.[81] Brunner's view, which classifies folk religions into the scheme of general revelation and determines the contrast between mediator faith and intermediate loose religiosity, often appears artificial and forcibly constructed. In the attempt to win Christianity for itself in

---

78. Brunner, *Mittler* [*Mediator*], 13ff, 372–73.

79. Brunner, *Mittler* [*Mediator*], 371ff.

80. Brunner, *Mittler* [*Mediator*], 6.; see Fichte, *Anweisung zum seligen Leben*, 485.

81. Brunner, *Mittler* [*Mediator*], 3ff.

all cases, his argumentation is the same as that of the old apologetics. The following sentence is characteristic of this theoretical construction:

> Revelation, as the unique-historical, is something that by its very nature can either never happen or can only happen once.[82]

According to Brunner, only the Christian faith recognizes revelation as something historical concrete in the sense of strict uniqueness and singularity.[83] With this immense triad that spans all world history, intellectual history, and salvation history, Brunner has captured the truth of natural revelation, as well as all truth, and traced it back to Christ:

> All truth is ultimately Christ-truth. What is true is true through him. Only the metaphysical, not the historical, saves: the Logos, who was in the beginning.[84]

In the "vulgar rationalism of the Enlightenment," Brunner sees an initial clear rejection of the view that all general revelation should replace the special revelation.[85] Similarly, Wegscheider also holds such an understanding of revelation and the teaching of Jesus.[86] Julius August Ludwig Wegscheider is considered the main representative of rationalistic theology. He is also influenced by Kant, striving to establish the connection between morality and religion and thus to ground religion itself as rational. His main work, published in 1825 and cited by Brunner, is considered the classic dogma of rationalism.[87]

"Only natural revelation" is considered by Wegscheider to be the true manifestation of God.[88] According to him, it provides

---

82. Brunner, *Mittler* [*Mediator*], 8.
83. Brunner, *Mittler* [*Mediator*], 7.
84. Brunner, *Mittler* [*Mediator*], 372–73.
85. Brunner, *Mittler* [*Mediator*], 24.
86. Brunner, *Mittler* [*Mediator*], 25.
87. See Betz et al., *Religion in Geschichte* 5, columns 1136–37.
88. Wegscheider, *Institutiones theologiae christianae dogmaticae*, 42, cited by Brunner: see *Mittler* [*Mediator*], 25.

insight into the principles of true religion. Natural theology asks about the universal features of humanity and creation that on the one hand reveal something of God's being and on the other hand do not detract from God's revelation. For Brunner, the positive aspect of this is that Jesus deserves credit for establishing clearer principles than any other human being and thus promoting the religious education of humankind.[89] It is surprising that Brunner allows Wegscheider's statement about the pedagogical function of the person of Christ to be valid as a possibility. He also sees it positively to speak of Jesus Christ as the exemplary human being, as God originally intended, the archetype of humanity. And if it is true that only where a person recognizes their distance from God, becomes aware of their humanity as their lost proximity to God, and is led into crisis by their best efforts, can the other, truly saving, be heard again, then the opposite also applies.

Thus, Brunner takes the side of humanity, recognizing its ability to know God or at least ask the right questions about God. He calls for the pursuit of naturally existing bridges of faith and proves that he believes humans are conditionally free, personal beings in a relationship with God in the interest of living faith.

"The Word of God cannot fill an empty space, but rather it seeks entry into a house that is already occupied. It cannot establish itself in any other way than by allowing itself to enter a dialogue with the spirits that are already present. It must make room for itself at their expense." Brunner does not want to merge theology into anthropology. He argues that the second task of theology is contentious, namely of "eristic nature."[90]

Later in his work "The Other Task of Theology," Brunner suggests the connection between the image of humanity and a Christology that understands Jesus' humanity not only as a veil but also as a revelation of the divine nature of God. He describes the revelation of God in Jesus Christ as "a consequence (of God) itself a pedagogical act, the act of condescending to our understanding."[91]

---

89. Brunner, *Mittler* [*Mediator*], 25.
90. See Brunner, "andere Aufgabe der Theologie," 255, 260, 273.
91. Brunner, "andere Aufgabe der Theologie."

SECOND PART

Thus, in terms of his human experience, Jesus is primarily a revelation and not a veil of God. According to the typically Calvinistic idea adopted by Brunner, God approaches humans both in Jesus Christ and in the sacraments in a pedagogical way adapted to human understanding.[92] Therefore, it is not in keeping with God's pedagogical action to create as great a gap as possible between the humanity of Jesus and the divine person of Jesus Christ, but rather to connect the humanity of Jesus with this person as an observable expression of the person of Christ with this person (hypostatic union). Brunner expressly cites Calvin as his authority for his understanding of nature, humanity, and Christ in his subsequent work *Natur und Gnade*.[93] Therefore, Christ must be recognized and honored as the greatest religious leader, teacher, and motivator of humanity,[94] even though divine worship towards him is inappropriate since he is essentially human, like us. Only his

---

92. See Calvin, *Institutio Christianae Religionis*, 2:16.2–3; *Ioannis Calvini* 3:483–84; *Institutio Christianae Religionis* 4.14.3.; *Ioannis Calvini* 5:260, 18ff.

93. See Brunner, *Natur und Gnade* (quote from "Nature"), for a discussion with Karl Barth, 28n1. In *Natur und Gnade*, Brunner responds to Barth with six theses: "1) While Barth claims that the image of God in humans has been completely erased by sin, Brunner distinguishes between a material imago Dei, which humans have indeed lost—referring to original righteousness, and a formal imago, which they still possess . . . and that is why humans can be addressed in preaching. 2) Since the world is God's creation, it is also a revelation, that is, a self-communication of God. That sin makes humans blind to it, or at least clouds their vision, does not mean that there can be no knowledge of God at all . . . 3) With regard to the fallen world, Brunner speaks of a preserving grace of God, which can only be properly understood in the light of the revelation of Christ, but which is already effective beforehand, for example, by warding off the most extreme consequences of sin. 4) This primarily includes orders such as marriage and the state, which can only be realized properly in faith, but which were created and managed as natural orders based on instinct and reason, and which can be respected as holy orders by humans. 5) Thus, there remains for the sinful human a humanity, primarily a power of speech and responsibility, which is a prerequisite for understanding the Gospel. 6) When the Scripture speaks of the death of the old man and a radical new creation, it refers only to the material, not the formal consideration of humanity" (Kreck, *Basic Decisions*, 119–21).

94. Brunner, *Mittler* [*Mediator*], 26.

teachings are divine, not his person;[95] "only where this truly saving (aspect) makes itself perceptible to him does that self-knowledge occur."[96]

Brunner notes here: Does not human experience itself have its foundation in revelation and only find its meaning in it? Does it not also have its "Prius" in the divine address?[97] Brunner explicitly asks about the human before and in faith "from faith itself," thus he asks about the conditions that lie within the process of faith itself. It must be said: "Christ is the truth of all philosophy and religion," not "everything that is true in philosophy and religion is Christ."

Therefore, Plato must be understood from John, not John from Plato, since Platonism is a "separated truth of Christ."[98]

2.2.3. Brunner's Critique of the Understanding of Special Revelation in "Contemporary Modern Theology"

Brunner's polemic begins with a reference to the fundamental opposition between the biblical and the general concept of revelation. The latter is the origin of all forms of immanent religion.[99] In contrast, the revelation of God is only the experience of the non-experienceability of God, the *"totaliter aliter"* breaking in "vertically from above," the unavailability of the external word! Only this waiting, given in the uniqueness and uniqueness of divine self-revelation, is the basis and object of faith and theology. *Verbum est pricipium primum!*[100]

---

95. Brunner, *Mittler* [*Mediator*], 26.

96. See Brunner, *Religionsphilosophie protestantischer Theologie*, 8.57. Brunner begins by explaining that there cannot be a philosophy of religion in the true sense on the basis of Christian theology since theology deals not with religion but with revelation. Nevertheless, Brunner understands revelation as a response to human openness: to their questions and their need for life (Brunner, *Religionsphilosophie protestantischer Theologie*, 5, 8.).

97. Brunner, *Religionsphilosophie protestantischer Theologie*, 8.57.

98. Brunner, *Mittler* [*Mediator*], 180–81, 372–73.

99. For a summary, see Brunner's *Mittler* [*Mediator*], chapters 1–5.

100. Brunner, *Religionsphilosophie protestantischer Theologie*, 2.

SECOND PART

This misunderstanding of human reality and its possibilities is demonstrated by Brunner in a detailed discussion of the idealistic, "humanistic concept of revelation in philosophy and theology": The religion of our classics is a middleless religion.[101] Behind it lies the conviction of continuity, the immediate relationship between God and man, in which man is permitted to make God present to himself. According to the credo of this self-understanding, human and divine consciousness become immediately one, the divine background shimmers through all appearances, nature becomes divine vision, history becomes revelation, human intellectual history becomes history of revelation; God is revealed not in the mediator man, but in humanity, and thus also in the individual human being. He reveals himself in the depth of human spirit.[102] The misunderstanding of God, which is expressed in the idealistic-humanistic concept of revelation, is at the same time a misunderstanding of human existence.

According to Brunner, the views of theological rationalism do not differ significantly from those of mystical-romantic theology. Brunner dealt with this in his early writings and published a comprehensive critique of it after his turn to dialectical theology.[103] In his *Mediator*, he adopted the Christological part of this critique without significant changes.[104] His starting point is Schleierm-

---

101. Brunner, *Religionsphilosophie protestantischer Theologie*, 9ff., 21ff., 49ff., 77ff., 98ff.

102. Brunner, *Religionsphilosophie protestantischer Theologie*; also see *Anfänge der dialektischen Theologie* 1:263, 310–11.

103. 238. See Brunner, *Mystik und Wort*.

104. See K. Barth, "Brunner's Schleiermacherbuch," 49–64; also see Barth's circular letter from March 1924, in which he asks whether Brunner has realized "before which unprecedented historical abyss we stand after this tower (referring to Schleiermacher) has been blown up from the basement into the air?" (Barth and Thurneysen, *Briefwechsel*, 2:235). Also see Krause and Müller, *TRE*, 8:238: "The turning point in theology that began with Barth's Romans, he vigorously supported in order to regain Christianity as a living force. Barth's priority was established, but he was the most gifted and eager collaborator, although not the systematic theologian of dialectical theology, as he was soon acclaimed for his philosophical education and clear presentation skills (Gestrich, BHTh 52, 28). It was also wrong to constantly mention him

acher's insistence on a general religion, a so-called "religion within religions,"[105] in which there is no place for the singularity or even absoluteness of the Christian religion. For Brunner, the absoluteness of the Christian faith means holding onto the uniqueness, unsurpassability, and finality of God's self-revelation in Jesus Christ. According to Schleiermacher, a fundamental surpassing of general revelation by Jesus seems to be excluded. However, Brunner maintains that Jesus is "the sublime author of the most glorious thing that exists in religion so far."[106]

Just as in rationalistic theology Jesus was only a human teacher of a divine doctrine, in this case he appears only as a human example for the pious and as the human instigator of the feeling for God.[107] If the religious feeling has also come alive in other people through Jesus, he increasingly recedes as a mediator. In an earlier work, *Experience, Knowledge, and Faith*, Brunner had already attributed no significance to religious feeling for the revelation of God. Therefore, he is no longer interested in Jesus Christ, the revelation of God, for his religious inner life. In fact, he sees this attempt to explore, with the aim of finding God in him, as an act of profound human unbelief.[108] Therefore, Brunner

---

and Barth in the same breath, even though in the English-speaking world, he was held almost exclusively. It would also be too simplistic to call him the ethicist and Barth the dogmatist of the new direction. For one thing, he was barely involved in the fundamental questions of their dialectic, which others considered essential. Barth and Thurneysen expressed reservations about him in their correspondence. On the other hand, despite the great common breakthrough, he maintained his independence and often turned away from Barth, later also from Gogarten. With Barth, creation would be given less weight than redemption, and with Gogarten, redemption would be given less weight than creation. Brunner, on the other hand, attempted a synthesis, adhering more to Barth's foundation, which, however, became too institutional for him: Barth was the man of the church for the churches, while I am more like a missionary; and in this intention lay his advocacy of the point of connection, for which he was branded as a relapse into natural theology."

105. Brunner, *Mittler*, 27.

106. See Friedrich Schleiermacher, *Über die Religion*, fifth essay, quoted in Brunner, *Mittler*, 29.

107. Brunner, *Mittler*, 29.

108. Brunner, *Erlebnis, Erkenntnis und Glaube*, 10, 56

SECOND PART

rejects the relationship he used in his earlier work of Jesus as a "religious genius" and "religious hero,"[109] as they express the rejection of Jesus' divinity. These concepts assume that Jesus' divinity can be directly derived from his extraordinary human disposition or religious ability.[110]

Does everyone who finds themselves in a relationship of dependencies have religion? To whom does this feeling of dependence refer? In addition to God, the universe also appears as a reference point for dependence. Theology cannot consist solely of a description and analysis of human religious acts but must provide a positive and definitive description of human action and his God to achieve its purpose.[111] As every religion cultivates only this one feeling, it is insignificant to which specific religion an individual belongs.[112] For Brunner, theology breaks down into two completely diverse parts:[113] one part is the doctrine of the essence of religion and of Christian faith as the concretization of this essence, thus the idea of Jesus as the special but not strictly unique mediator and stimulator of religious essence. The other part is the doctrine of the unpredictable and derivable only from itself self-revelation of God and the redemption of humans in and through Jesus Christ, thus the idea of Jesus as the only true mediator essentially different from all other humans, including religious heroes. According to Brunner, the fundamentally same danger of relativizing the mediation of Jesus Christ also comes from the theology of Albrecht Ritschl and his followers, as they, like theological rationalism and romantic mysticism, are based on a general concept of religion.[114]

The relationship between Jesus and the content of this general concept of religion can easily be understood as twofold: on the one

109. Brunner, *Erlebnis, Erkenntnis und Glaube*, 10, 16, 20, 34, 56.

110. Brunner, *Erlebnis, Erkenntnis und Glaube*, 56.

111. See Brunner, *Mystik und Wort*, 367–68; see also Thielicke, *Prolegomena* [*Introduction*], 34: Schleiermacher does not give a clear answer to this in his speeches.

112. Brunner, *Mittler* [*Mediator*], 28.

113. Brunner, *Mittler* [*Mediator*], 33.

114. Brunner, *Mittler* [*Mediator*], 34.

hand, Jesus is considered the originator of the idea of the moral purpose, thus he is the first human in whom this idea shines forth in full clarity; on the other hand, Jesus personally and completely represents this idea through the identity of his will and actions with the idea of God's purposeful will, absolute love.[115]

Brunner now emphasizes as much as everything in the Christian faith is based on the fundamental contrast to the nonmediate general religion, he does not deny that "traces of truth in all religions and traces of God in all being and thinking must be recognized."[116] If the uniqueness of God's self-revelation in Christ is taken seriously, Christians can only believe in general or natural revelation. This revelation can only be recognized as "broken," its truth is neither denied nor affirmed, but includes an awareness of the distortion and perversion of this truth, which has lost its original meaning. With this conceptually and materially still unsatisfactory determination of the relationship, Brunner connects to the thinking model he had already presented in *Experience, Knowledge and Faith*, which led him to speak of the "preliminary halftruth of experience and knowledge religion." It always served him to characterize the difficult-to-define fact that something is not true but also not simply untrue. According to Brunner, sin means "sensuality," not destruction, but perversion of the original. That is why all quantitative determinations of the still-existing original are something little, a remnant of the original—unsuitable.

The relationship between origin and perversion is not quantitative but dialectical, because it concerns a spiritual, not a natural relationship, not almost complete elimination but contradiction.[117] In any case, one must agree with Brunner's presentation of the

---

115. Brunner, *Mittler* [*Mediator*], 37–38.

116. Brunner, *Mittler* [*Mediator*], 13.

117. See Brunner, *Offenbarung und Vernunft* [*Revelation and Reason*] 5.90. His work *Offenbarung und Vernunft* leaves a somewhat ambiguous impression, insofar as essential positions of Brunner's against Barth are retracted. Although Barth's strong attack on natural theology and the *analogia entis* could not persuade Brunner to abandon his aim of establishing connections, he now tried to implement it for culture. In this attempt, the demarcation from reason became sharper than one could have expected in the mid-1930s.

danger posed to faith in Christ by subsuming it under the principles of a religion of feeling.[118] Although Jesus is the author of the highest moral idea and thus the founder of Christianity, the person of Jesus as mediator is insignificant, as it only means the revelation of the truth that is valid in itself at a particular moment, but not the person as enduring truth itself.[119] Similarly, according to Brunner, Ritschl's explanation that Christ perfectly represented the idea of divine purpose is problematic.[120] He claims that in Jesus' professional work, "the Word of God is a human person."[121] This is clear from Ritschl's following sentence: "If a second person could be shown to be materially equal to him in grace and fidelity, he would nevertheless be in historical dependence on Christ, and thus formally unequal to him."[122] In contrast, tradition wants to hear in the professional, thus humanly perceptible, work of Jesus Christ the Word of God as the second divine person, as the personal mystery of the Son of God. Regarding Ritschl's reversal of the understanding of the person of Jesus in relation to traditional dogmatic statements, it may be conceded that his extremely critical presentation of Christology cannot be entirely wrong. Thus, Jesus here, despite Ritschl's talk of the divinity of Jesus, is only the bearer of the divine idea, but neither a divine person nor a true mediator.[123]

Even in Harnack, revelation appears as something universal, always and everywhere valid.[124] The confession of Christ as the only mediator is missing both in the theology of Harnack and in that of his intellectual predecessors Wegscheider, Schleiermacher, and Ritschl. Although the so-called history of religion school is very interested in the historical phenomena of religion, it does not

---

118. Brunner, *Mystik und Wort*, 94.

119. Brunner, *Mittler*, 41–42.

120. Brunner, *Mittler*, 41–42.

121. Albrecht Ritschl, *positive Entwicklung der Lehre*, 426, quoted by Brunner, *Mittler* [*Mediator*], 42.

122. Brunner, *Mittler* [*Mediator*], 438.

123. See D-S, 3026: Ritschl's statement violates the "atreptos" of Chalcedon; the Word of God does not transform into a human person.

124. Brunner, *Mittler* [*Mediator*], 43.

assign them any decisive importance.[125] According to it, the ultimate binding force for faith has nothing historically concrete, but a universally valid essence, whether it is the "irrational experience of the holy" as in Rudolf Otto or the "experience of the divine presence" as in Ernst Troeltsch, which theologically interpreted forces acceptance of a religious a priori.[126] However, the absoluteness of Christianity stands or falls with the absoluteness of Christ.[127]

If modern theology in its various directions holds on to a general revelation and does not acknowledge a particular revelation, it reduces Christology to a treatise on the humanity of Jesus, which Brunner rightly recognized. However, he did not examine carefully enough whether, under certain conditions, such as a fundamentally more positive assessment of the human idea of God, a bridge to traditional Christological confession could not be built from Schleiermacher's theology, and thus still a priori blocks a modern path to the ancient faith. However, the theological anthropology later developed by Brunner already shows some signs of this in *Mittler*.[128] In a sense, the prerequisites are given when humans become aware of their own existential distress and experience the limits of their possibilities. "God can only be recognized from the depths." Nevertheless, humans only recognize their guilt "through the message of reconciliation." The real knowledge of sin "is only possible on the basis of revelation." And only through the message of God's revelation in Christ will they become "aware of the questionable nature of their natural knowledge of God."[129]

---

125. Brunner, *Mittler* [*Mediator*], 45.

126. Brunner, *Mittler* [*Mediator*], 46.

127. This refers not to a dogmatic, but to a phenomenological connection between revelation, religion, and reason.

128. See, for example, *Man in Revolt* (1937); *Wahrheit als Begegnung* [*Truth as Encounter*] (1938). While Brunner focused on the anthropological problem in *Man in Revolt*, he now addressed the relationship between Christianity and culture in his next work, *Offenbarung und Vernunft* [*Revelation and Reason*].

129. Brunner, *Mittler* [*Mediator*], 115, 126, 266–67.

SECOND PART

2.3. TURN TO ERISTIC (1928)

2.3.1. Continuity in Brunner's Thinking

As the predominant characteristic of the actual biblical fundamental category of the period after 1927, on the one hand, the question of the proclamation of God to man can be considered, but on the other hand, also the increasingly strong emphasis on the personal correspondence between God and man. The preface to the second volume of Brunner's *Dogmatics* initially confirms this judgment. The content of this work, the doctrine of creation and redemption, is referred to by Brunner there as a first attempt to systematically apply "the rediscovery of the 'I and Thou' by Ebner and Buber" as well as the new insights of the Scripture *Truth as Encounter* (1938) to Brunner's thought that has changed and developed in many ways during this period.[130] His thoughts became best known through the continued engagement with Karl Barth in the field of anthropology.

However, it will be shown that the turn in Brunner's thinking did not only take place with the turn to Eristic but that the prerequisites are already recognizable in his dialectical early writings. As far as dialectical theology means nothing other than holding on to the paradox of the revelation event, Brunner has always called his theology dialectical. But if it is understood as the programmatic community with friends, the break is evident at the latest in Brunner's formulation of the "other task of theology" as a theological program in 1929. As soon as the period of "Eristic" is mentioned, it is important to note that Brunner wanted to understand this term in the context of dialectics.

---

130. Brunner completed his life's work with the three-volume *Dogmatik*. Brunner also wanted his dogmatics to be understood by non-theologians with a thinking mind (*christliche Lehre von Gott*, xi). He does not start with thoughts from his eristic theology, but with the doctrine of revelation, which he determines as personal revelation of Christ. From him, the preceding revelations, the primordial revelation and the Old Testament revelation differ in that God has not yet revealed himself in personal self-presentation.

EMIL BRUNNER'S INTEGRATION OF FAITH AND REASON

In his work *Truth as Encounter*, Emil Brunner remains true to the approach of the three-personhood and word-hood of God, which was already predominant in the *Mediator*. From there, he develops the insight that there is essentially a relationship of personal correspondence between God and humanity.[131] Just as we only become human persons when someone addresses us, accepts us, and introduces us into human society, we gain our personhood, self-knowledge, and responsibility for the world only through the creative love and sovereign claim of God.[132]

Brunner emphasizes this rational and contemporary approach even more than Friedrich Gogarten and Rudolf Bultmann,[133] drawing on sources such as Augustine, Pascal, Hamann, Kierkegaard, Ebner, Buber, and Heidegger.[134] At the same time, he remains committed to his philosophical framework, Neo-Kantianism. In *Truth as Encounter*, he outlines human personhood as a responsive actuality.[135] Truth is not within us; it is historically mediated to us, enters our loneliness, and breaks open the prison of the self. Truth emerges through communicative speech acts. In the word, a Thou shares itself with us and thereby opens reality for us. Historicity, linguistic ability, and humor are thus grounded in the love that is given to us. Only through this love granted to us, does our responsive actuality emerge, and thus, through the exchange between individuals, freedom for life arises. The love that is given to

---

131. See Brunner, *Wahrheit als Begegnung* [*Truth as Encounter*], 80. With "fides quarens intellectum," Barth had completed the determined turn to theological objectivism. Nevertheless, the subject of theology is still the self-interpreting revelation, which man only has to contemplate. Brunner, on the other hand, in *Wahrheit als Begegnung*, grasps Christian truth as personal encounter truth between God and man. Thus, he tries to overcome theological subjectivism and objectivism.

132. See Weber, *Grundlagen der Dogmatik* [*Foundations of Dogmatics*] 590–91: "Because God is a person, therefore man is a person; that is: because God steps out of himself and speaks, in this and therein man is a responsive and destined being to respond."

133. See Hummel, *Theologische Anthropologie*, 39–80 (Bultmann), 80–131 (Gogarten).

134. Brunner, *Man in Revolt*, 18, 498; *Truth as Encounter*, 6off.

135. Brunner, *Truth as Encounter*, 35ff.

us precedes us in the guidance of life areas, and our response will lead us back to love:

> Man is only human to the extent that he is in love.[136]

Brunner's theses are, of course, not formulated as human biological or social pedagogical insights but are strictly theological statements to which human insight cannot penetrate on its own, remaining marked by hubris. True humanity, grounded in this call, is being-in-love and is received in faith. God's creation, true humanity, is an act of God that can only be completed in the responding act of human beings. Humanity is created in such a way that it must respond in accordance with or in opposition to the divine will, whether it wants to or not.[137]

For Brunner, theology exists in the tension between two poles: the divine message and the human situation. Its task is therefore determined both as

> the self-reflection of the Christian community on the basis, meaning and content of the message given and entrusted to it,[138]

and as the confrontation of this message with the contemporary situation. Only in this double orientation, in its God and human reference, does theology gain its legitimacy. If it does not base its statements on revelation as the substance and criterion of all its assertions, then it gives up on itself. If, in its discourse on this

---

136. Brunner, *Truth as Encounter*, 77.

137. Brunner, *christliche Lehre von Schöpfung*, 86.

138. In his program of eristic theology, Brunner aimed at the connection between message and situation, between the Word of God and human existence, between revelation and reason, between church and world, which allowed him to make his contribution ecumenically effective as an ethicist and in his later works as a dogmatist. He traced his "theological work back to the early influence of Christoph Blumhardt as the fruit of his seed" (Brunner, *Dogmatik*, 3:31; Ebeling, ZThK 66, 356–57). See also Karl Barth, *Kirkliche Dogmatik*, 2:29: "It would not be a serious perception of this reality if it did not immediately want to become understanding. It would not be credere at all if it did not press toward intelligere. It is about God's revelation in this reality, thus about God's relationship to us, about his reality that concerns us."

revelation, it does not consciously aim to address and engage with the understanding of humanity in a concrete way, then it poses its own question of meaning.[139]

For Brunner, the aim was to bring the claim character of revelation more strongly to the fore, to illustrate the decision-making character of faith more clearly, and to address and hold humans accountable for their responsibility and being before God. Brunner sought a *theologia ad hominem*, a "total turning towards humanity in God's mission."[140]

> Anyone who claims that one cannot take human beings seriously if one takes God seriously or that one cannot look at the human being when one is concerned with "the cause" has something other in mind than the Gospel of Jesus Christ. The more seriously one takes God, the more seriously one takes human beings, the more passionately one struggles for human beings. Proclamation is not an anonymous calling out of a truth into the world—now let whoever wants to hear it. Instead, it is the discovery of Him (Jesus) from God and an obligation to God.[141]

Brunner first expressed this view in his much-debated essay of 1929 on "The Other Task of Theology." According to him, theology has a double task: (1) the explicit exposition of revelation as the self-reflection of the church on the witness entrusted to it (dogmatics) and (2) the confrontation with the world's knowledge and the self-understanding of the pre-believing human being (polemics).[142]

Brunner calls this polemical theology, "*theologia ad hominem*," Eristic. While "man before God" was indeed the constant theme of Brunner's theology, its direction has fundamentally changed in relation to the changing fronts. One could say that Brunner unfolded this theme in the two periods of his work towards its two sides. Thus, the point of contact where faith and

139. Brunner, *Revelation and Reason*, 410.
140. Brunner, *Revelation and Reason*, 410.
141. Brunner, "Andere Aufgabe der Theologie," especially 259–60.
142. Brunner, *Man in Revolt*, preface, ix.

unbelief meet, i.e., the starting point, is a question of anthropology, the understanding of one's own existence, regardless of whether it is supported by the question of God or not. Nevertheless, Brunner starts with a pre-Christian revelation:

> That even the unbeliever is not without a relationship with God and therefore responsible, and that this responsibility is not invalidated but rather claimed by even the most radical assertion of grace: that is the main idea of my book.[143]

Therefore, Eristic takes the form of a conversation between a believer and a non-believer. It addresses their questions, "it comes to them in their distress, their helplessness, their skepticism, and their longing."[144]

Brunner was and remained a dialectician in the sense that he recognized it as a necessary form of thought for theology to reflect the contradiction between God and man, revelation and reason, grace, and responsibility. This thinking is a more distant, often repeating one that loves the once-coined formulation. But despite all its rationality, it aims to be understood as "believing thinking."[145]

2.3.2. The Transformation to the I-Thou Philosophy

The similarities between Brunner and Barth in their understanding of the Word of God during the period of 1919 to 1927 are particularly easy to identify. In his dialectical work *Experience, Knowledge, and Faith*, Brunner describes the revelation event, like Karl Barth, as a human tracing of the Word of God brought about by the Holy Spirit, in which God is the only active speaker and man is merely the membrane of divine speech. Faith is

---

143. Brunner, *Christliche Lehre von Gott*, 110; Brunner does not clearly distinguish between eristic and missionary theology, which is why it will be dispensed with here.

144. Brunner, *Christliche Lehre von Gott*, 6.

145. Brunner, *Mittler* [*Mediator*], 94.

simply repeating what the divine truth declares. By awkwardly tracing the divine Word, man traces himself into faith.[146]

Therefore, the Word of God establishes a dialogue with itself through and in man, but it is not an exchange between God and man in which man is an independent conversational partner.

Since around 1923, Brunner's understanding of the divine-human dialogue changed with his explicit reference to Ferdinand Ebner's thoughts.[147] To illustrate this change, a brief review of the philosophical prerequisites and foundations of Brunner's thinking is necessary. A fundamental realization emerges here with Brunner's question about the sought-after relationship between the transcendental objectivity of the object of faith and its existential appropriation, which anticipates the difficulty of the relationship between revelation and faith.[148] The significance of this insight by Ebner and Buber, which is only briefly hinted at here, should not be underestimated, as the self-effectiveness of the Thou-world (the encounter) they discovered compared to the It-world (the fact) opens up a new dimension for thinking.[149] Barth warns early on against linking the so-called I-Thou philosophy with theology, as this science gives man too much natural power for a relationship with God.[150]

On the other hand, in Brunner, a certain disposition towards dialogical thinking can be assumed; in the early phase of

---

146. Brunner, *Mystik und Wort*, 395n3; see also Gestrich, *Neuzeitliches Denken*; see Ebner, *Wort und geistigen Realitäten*, 90–91, 128–30; also see Buber, *Ich und Du*, 97, 100, 110–11.

147. Salakka, *Person und Offenbarung*, highlights Brunner's religious philosophical origins.

148. Brunner refers to his origins in Kierkegaard in several writings: "Basic Problem of Philosophy in Kant and Kierkegaard" (1924), "Encounter with Kierkegaard" (1929), and " Botschaft Sören Kierkegaards" ["Message of Kierkegaard"] (1930).

149. See the systematic development of this insight in K. Heim's ontology of the dimensions of the real in *Glaube und Denken* (1931).

150. See Cullberg's account of the history of the Ich-Du philosophy and its impact on theology in "Du und die Wirklichkeit" (1933).

his theology, he, like Ferdinand Ebner, was a follower of Bergson's philosophy of life.[151] This common starting point suggests that a direct path to dialogical thinking led from there. The openness of a philosophy of life to dialogical thinking is obvious since human life never arises from "solitude" but from the relationship between two people. Human life, therefore, is always founded on human dialogue in the broadest sense and is then realized in its existence in the most diverse relationships. Aristotle already expressed this through the classical definition that man is a *zoon politikon*.[152]

However, while Ebner dealt with Feuerbach's philosophy of I-Thou, Brunner did not.[153] Feuerbach opposes Hegel's idea to life in its immediate concreteness and tries to bring the identity-philosophical approach of Hegel to absurdity by asserting the I-Thou relationship.[154]

Therefore, Gestrich's judgment that Brunner diverged from Karl Barth not only due to his growing reception of F. Ebner's philosophy of word and person in 1923, but also due to his earlier engagement with Bergson's philosophy, is to be agreed with to the extent that it created a disposition in Brunner for dialogical thinking that deviated from Barth.[155] After 1927, in his work *Protestant Theology's Philosophy of Religion*, written after *The Mediator*, Brunner claimed that the Holy Spirit's work leading to faith is perceptible

> where the ego is no longer a self-acting subject but only a stage, no longer speaking for itself, but only resonance for God's speech, where subjectivity is consumed by the truth, not only allowing itself to be grasped but also grasping itself.[156]

---

151. See Ebner, *Wort und geistigen Realitäten*, 1131–32.

152. See Aristotle, *Eth. Nik.* 1.5 1097b 11; and *Politik* 1.6:1278b 19, 214, 288.

153. Ebner, *Schriften* [*Writings*], 2:1165n12–13, 1170n40.

154. See Hirschberger, *Geschichte der Philosophie* 2:470–71; see also Gestrich, *Neuzeitliches Denken*, 170.

155. Gestrich, *Neuzeitliches Denken*, 33.

156. Brunner, *Religionsphilosophie protestantischer Theologie*, 12.

In this context, Brunner refers to Calvin,[157] but despite this, Calvin never understood the work of the Spirit in man to consume subjectivity or personality, but rather that man as a subject is elevated to God despite his sinfulness.[158]

How can man be a free, decision-making "Thou" before God if the working of the Holy Spirit in man consumes subjectivity? Only in his work "The Other Task of Theology" (1929) does Brunner understand the word of God not only as a purely monological word going from God to God, but also as the basis of a true dialogue between God and man, which requires a free response from man. Brunner takes into account the anthropological consequences arising from his new, more dialogical than dialectical view of man in another book from 1929, entitled *The Unique and the Character of Existence*.[159] Once again, Brunner refers to the "being addressed and being spoken to" as a prerequisite for personal divine revelation.[160] In his book *The Message of Christ in the Struggle with Religions*, Brunner speaks of the inseparable connection between the two Christian concepts of revelation and faith.[161] According to Brunner, the comparison of Christian and non-Christian concepts of revelation and faith shows that Christian claims of revelation and Christian faith behave like "good conversational partners" and that whoever changes one of these partners changes the entire dialogue between God and man within Christianity.[162] By nature, human beings are capable of language, eloquence, responsiveness, and reason.[163]

---

157. See Ganoczy, *Ecclesia Ministrans*, 192; see Calvin, *Ioannis Calvini*, 53:435.

158. Ganoczy, *Ecclesia Ministrans*.

159. See Brunner, *Blätter für Deutsche Philosophie* 3:265–82.

160. Brunner, *Blätter für Deutsche Philosophie* 3:271.

161. See Brunner, "Christusbotschaft im Kampf," especially 8–9.

162. Brunner, "Christusbotschaft im Kampf," especially 8–9.

163. See Brunner, "Frage nach dem 'Anknüpfungspunkt,'" 514; see also Krause and Müller, *TRE*, 8:239: "That was already programmed in the inaugural lecture in 1925, linked with an attack on the sinfully twisted intellectuality. If thinking reaches a point where humans no longer know anything on their own, the question of the starting point becomes a problem of theology, the

Man is naturally able to speak, articulate, respond, and reason, which distinguishes him permanently from animals and the rest of creation and is not erased by sin.[164] The term "starting point" became the catchword for the controversy. On the one hand, Brunner was accused of creating dangerous conditions for the "natural" man to reach divine salvation grace and therefore making compromises with *sola gratia*. On the other hand, Brunner accused his opponents of unjustifiable unkindness in breaking bridges with today's non-churchgoing people that God had left to the sinful man for faith in a false zeal for the glory of God.[165]

Brunner believes that he can rightfully claim that, like Barth, he is concerned with the entire truth of the Reformation message of God's sovereign grace election, justification by faith alone, the crucified Christ as the only savior of the world, and the Scripture as the only criterion of theology.[166] In his writing regarding a conversation with K. Barth, *Natur und Gnade*, Brunner attempted to show in the face of Barth's massive accusations that what Barth fought for was the same as what he wanted and meant; however, Barth drew false conclusions from his legitimate claims and wrongly accused those who did not follow him of betraying the cause.[167]

Therefore, Brunner was unjustly accused by Barth of subscribing to natural theology. Barth's misunderstanding arose from his confusion of the knowledge and the ontological foundation of a theological statement.[168] Brunner also denied that the "natural

---

fundamental question of his eristic theology, but it ensures ontological and current references to the changing consciousness of time (see "Frage nach dem 'Anknüpfungspunkt,'" 509–12). The commonality with Barth was broken on this problem, and Schleiermacher's actual concern remained unintentionally preserved in Brunner's solution. Therefore, at its core, Brunner's eristic is also irenic" (see Gestrich, *Neuzeitliches Denken*, 353).

164. Brunner, "Frage nach dem 'Anknüpfungspunkt,'" 520–21; see Brunner, *Natur und Gnade*, 10–11.
165. Brunner, "andere Aufgabe," 273.
166. Brunner, *Natur und Gnade*, 5.
167. Brunner, *Natur und Gnade*, 4.
168. Brunner, *Natur und Gnade*, 41, 57: "I am . . . of the opinion with Barth

man can obtain the latter [ontological foundation] in any valid way on his own: We do not recognize the revelation of creation from the world, but from the revelation. But we recognize through revelation the Creator in the world, if it is His creation."[169] Furthermore, Brunner emphasized that "the message of the church does not have sources and norms, such as revelation and reason, or the Word of God and history, . . . commandment and order."

There was no disagreement between him and Barth, except that Barth believed there was one.[170] "I feel so much like Barth's ally, even in what he believed he had to accuse me of, that I was able to easily overlook the misunderstanding."[171]

Finally, Barth could not deny that there was a problem in the relationship between revelation and reason, Christianity and culture, commandment, and order, which needed clarification.[172] Barth's "Response to Emil Brunner" was a harsh, uncompromising "No,"[173] condemning Brunner's approach from its inception.

---

that there is no legitimate knowledge of God through the use of the analogy principle, but only knowledge gained from Jesus Christ."

169. "It is the task of our theological generation to rediscover the right natural theology" (Brunner, *Natur und Gnade*, 44).

170. Brunner, *Natur und Gnade*, 6.

171. Brunner, *Natur und Gnade*, 3.

172. Brunner, *Natur und Gnade*, 6.

173. K. Barth, "Nein!"

The view expressed by Barth against Brunner in the polemic "No!" is absent in his later theology: "Creation orders" (*Kirchliche Dogmatik* II-2, 153–57; III-4, 201, §39ff.). Barth argues there against the doctrine of creation orders. It is based on presumptions at first and, with its abstraction from the revealed Word of God, with its reference to the obscure great "reality," and with its credulity regarding the human ability to derive usable knowledge of God and our relationship to him from this obscure thing, it gives no reliable and no authentic answer to the question of the commanding God and the creature confronting him (III, §40). Furthermore, it separates the command of the Creator in the given structures from the command of the reconciler, which is thereby referred to the realm of interiority. In addition, it does not achieve the true God and the true human by dealing with the concepts of "Creator" and "creature" as if they were dealing with the concepts of "cause," "effect," and "causal nexus" (III, §41).

SECOND PART

> I understand "natural theology" to mean any . . . supposedly theological system, i.e., presenting itself as an interpretation of divine revelation, whose 'object is different from the revelation of God in Jesus Christ.[174]

Brunner had nothing else to say in response than "that I find nothing to retract in my explanations."[175] This resulted in a definitive end to the theological conversation. Looking back on what has been said so far, it is clear that it was solely the claim of the character of revelation or the responsibility of humanity in general that concerned Brunner in his efforts towards Barth. This was also what led him to adhere to a revelation of God in creation despite all opposition, and not any intended softening of *sola gratia*, any secret flirtation with natural theology, or any desire to rescue humanity's honor before God.[176] After 1928, Brunner saw theology as arising from the necessity of making a special connection and fulfilling another task, which is "to show, in addition to the thetic and explicative exposition of the correct meaning and coherence of individual articles of faith, how through the Word of God, human reason is partly revealed as a source of life-denying error, and partly fulfilled in its own, unfinished search (for God and for the correct self-understanding)."[177] These statements clearly indicate the dangerous path Brunner intended to take, as almost all of the characteristic and prominent teachings of his further theology were already contained in this approach.

2.3.3. The New Path towards the "Other Task of Theology"

The question of "religious knowledge" demands from the outset the development of the contrast between faith and experience, word and mysticism, in the demonstration of the relationship between the "I" and the "Thou," between word and response, between

---

174. K. Barth, "Nein!," 11–12.

175. Brunner, *Natur und Gnade*, v, foreword.

176. Brunner, *Man in Revolt*, ix, foreword.

177. Brunner, "andere Aufgabe der Theologie" ["Other Task of Theology"], 259–60.

faith and understanding. In the polar tension between content and form on one hand, and knowledge and act of existence on the other hand, two problem areas or dimensions of the concept of faith crystallize, to which almost all other problem relationships can be subordinated. For simplicity's sake, they shall be called here the "theological" and the "anthropological" dimensions of faith. The so-called theological dimension encompasses the relationship between God and man, that is, the objective and subjective moments of faith, faith as an objective act of grace and a subjective event of self-experience, as a spiritual effect and an appropriation act, as gift and task. The so-called anthropological dimension encompasses the tension within man himself, the contrast between the act of knowledge and existence, the intellectual and voluntaristic-existential moment in faith.[178] Correct theological thinking not only presupposes faith, but also leads to it. Brunner's intention is the continuous actualization of all his statements about faith:

> Therefore, Christian theology, which understands itself, can ultimately only exist as a theory of faith in a constant self-transcendence.

It is "theological discourse about why faith is not theoretical but existential,"[179] a factual reference to the personal character of faith, and only in that sense "adequate."[180] For Brunner, God as a transcendent person cannot be accessed by man through a monological, objectifying thinking about God, but only through the hearing and accepting of a word voluntarily spoken by God, in which God communicates who he is and who man is to whom he speaks. Faith is "the truly personal and truly person-creating relationship."[181]

---

178. Brunner, *christliche Lehre von Gott*, 48: "The difference between knowledge of faith and theological knowledge, which is so difficult to find yet so necessary, is not a difference in content but a difference in form of existence, in dimension of existence."

179. Brunner, *Mittler* [*Mediator*], 499.

180. Brunner, *christliche Lehre von Gott*, 98: "There is no theological existence, there is only theological thinking and believing existence."

181. Brunner, *Mittler* [*Mediator*], 238–39.

Faith is a personal relationship to God. God's total claim is at the same time the total demand on man. Therefore, the Bible always presents man as a responsible subject in relation to the word of God and understands the effectiveness of the word as a *sui generis* process that takes place as speaking and hearing, appropriation, and obedience.[182]

Faith calls man to decision, it makes a claim to be "the only truly personal decision; it is the decision in view of the divine personality, in view of the personal word and claim of God, the Lord, who in his addressing demands the decision that no law and no moral imperative can demand."[183]

Looking at faith and thus at God's intention, the humanity of Jesus is the revelation of the personality of God, the realization of God's community will, the shining forth of God's glory, the implementation of the divine world plan, the starting point of God in man and of man in God.[184] However, Brunner also states that man is called into existence by God as a free, decision-capable "thou," which is why "his life is realized according to his specific human, truly historical quality as a decisive answer to this call."[185]

According to Brunner, preaching and theological interpretation of the gospel must not ignore the knowledge of the non-Christian about God and themselves, but must connect with them to bring themselves to the fore.[186] Thus, Brunner explains, unbelievers are no longer neutral towards God, but have taken a stand towards God in their own way and related to that, have given themselves an answer to the question of the meaning of their existence.[187] For Brunner, the fact that theology cannot do without connection is demonstrated by the apologetics already practiced

---

182. Brunner, *Man in Revolt*, 551.
183. Brunner, *Mittler* [*Mediator*], 239.
184. Brunner, *Wahrheit als Begegnung*, 107.
185. Brunner, *Religionsphilosophie protestantischer Theologie*, 61.
186. Brunner, "andere Aufgabe," 262.
187. Brunner, "andere Aufgabe," 255.

by the church fathers, who engaged in a dialogical debate with the arguments of opponents of Christianity and tried to refute them.[188]

Brunner does not consider theology to be an objective science, since it appears to him primarily as biblical, existential, and systematic. Above all, it must separate itself from the axiom of reason, that self-occupation of modern emancipated reason that wants to establish itself *pro domo*. Brunner calls it a grand delusion.[189] Nevertheless, even a reason-critical theology requires reason, since it wants to understand the word of God:

> The relationship with God is not to be understood from reason, but reason is to be understood from the relationship with God, who is always given to man as the origin, but who is usually present only in lost knowledge, through his absence. He is recognized again in the middle of history, in the revelation of Jesus Christ.[190]

Based on his conviction of the connection between the word of God and humanity, Brunner even dares to describe some of Luther's statements, which seem to speak for determinism and thus for a lack of freedom and independence of humans before God, as "missteps that are understandable from a certain fighting situation, but should not be repeated." The statement frequently attributed to Luther that people are before God like "stumps and stones" does not directly result from the sentence in which Luther speaks of stumps and stones. It simply says:

> *Deinde ac si omnes homines essent trunci et lapides, andes in publico dicere, liberum arbitrium statur per loca scripturae, quae auxilium gratiae Dei commendant.*[191]

This statement is formulated in the subjunctive mood.[192] Brunner sees in this writing that Luther denies the possibility of humans making a free decision, a "free answer." Whether Luther's

---

188. Brunner, "andere Aufgabe," 258.
189. Brunner, "andere Aufgabe," 257.
190. Brunner, *Mensch im Widerspruch*, 93.
191. Luther, *De servo arbitrio*, 754. 36–38.
192. Brunner, "andere Aufgabe," 264.

attitude can be accurately described as determinism is another question. While Barth held fast to the barrier that is set for general insight when it wants to recognize the real human being, Brunner sees it differently: an unsparingly questioning reason can recognize the real human being to such an extent that it must recognize his self-contradictions (even if it still does not know that all contradictions ultimately come from a primordial contradiction, the loss of the center of being in God).

The true human being understands himself from God; he does not posit himself or reason as his own foundation.[193] This task, which Brunner calls "eristic"—the Greek term *eristike techne* means "art of disputation," and the task is to confirm or refute the worldly reasons for or against Christian faith—he considers equally important as the dogmatic task, while Barth regards it as secondary or completely rejects it.[194] Brunner defends the "eristic" task of theology against Barth's judgment by referring to "the act of preaching or the 'genuine sermon.'"[195]

Theology must demonstrate to what extent human reason is "revealed as a source of life-hostile error" through the Word of God.[196] It has to uncover the delusions of reason at the Word of God, which is essentially polemical. However, it must not remain stuck in the one-sidedness of the polemical. It must also focus on the event of proclamation in which humans experience themselves as understood and affirmed and liberated. This means: Theology, in perceiving its other task, must also show how through the Word of God, human reason is not only revealed as a source of error, but also brought to its own goal in its search. Theology has to "show reason its fulfillment in the Word of God."[197] Looking at preach-

---

193. Brunner, *Mensch im Widerspruch*, 93.

194. Regarding the meaning of the term "eristic," see Brunner, *Mensch im Widerspruch*, 266. Regarding Barth's evaluation of the "other" task of theology from Brunner's perspective, see "andere Aufgabe," 258, 274.

195. Brunner, *Mensch im Widerspruch*, 258, 259.

196. See Soden, "Theologie und Kirche," 398n1. "It is not about the psychological 'how' there, but about the decidedly theological question of in what way and in what respect man is responsive to the word of God."

197. Brunner, "andere Aufgabe," 257–58, 260.

ing, Brunner observes that a sermon that does not "address the listening person and draw them out of hiding," and does not attempt to touch the heart of the listener, can only be blind, standing at a distance from real human beings, and inhumane.[198]

The question whether the Eristic sought dialogue must be discussed against the background of the existential question that leads to anthropology, encompassing faith and unbelief. Especially when the Eristic pushes questions to existential abysses, they raise the question of humans' search for God, even if it is still veiled and unadmitted: "It is only because we are in God and know God that we can ask about Him."[199]

Nonetheless, Brunner remembers the many detours that dogmatic history has taken, such as those of the Semi-Pelagians, who had precisely determined what humans do by their own ability and what God does by grace. Brunner did not want to think like this, since he did not see the uncertainty as a residue of human performance before God—as an a priori—but saw God's presence incognito under the indeterminate search of humans. Brunner was aware of this dilemma but did not consider it a fundamental objection to what he called the "other task of theology." The knot that tightens here is present in every act of proclamation as an impossible possibility of what is happening, and yet it is resolved precisely in the act of proclamation.[200] The confrontation demanded here occurs in the obedience of faith. It is "a moment of the wonderful event of faith itself. . . . Right eristic theology, therefore, takes part in every event that we usually attribute only to preaching."[201]

Dialogical considerations can be found in Brunner's writings critical of Karl Barth's theology, which prepare for the transformation in Brunner's anthropological thinking. If one summarizes Brunner's statements about human beings as dialogical beings in these writings, one arrives at the following conclusion: they make

198. Brunner, "andere Aufgabe," 259, 275.
199. Brunner, "andere Aufgabe," 263.
200. Brunner, "andere Aufgabe," 260.
201. Brunner, "andere Aufgabe," 269.

humans responsible, capable of decision-making and therefore free subjects, or persons before God, thus creating a relationship of personal analogy between God and humans, i.e., a personal relationship and analogy.[202] What Brunner argues in *Natur und Gnade* is one thing that Barth sees as a threat to "the ultimate thing that must be guarded and defended in the Protestant Church."[203] In his essay on the first commandment as a "theological axiom" (1933), Barth attempted to counteract the deepening division in the camp of dialectical theology, but it was already too late for mutual understanding, and the open break was inevitable. The last year of the jointly founded journal *Between the Times* ended with Barth and Thurneysen's withdrawal, in which Barth also bid farewell to Brunner: "It so happened that I saw Emil Brunner, also counted among our group, pursuing a theology in and outside our journal that I increasingly could only evaluate as a return to the fleshpots of the land of Egypt, which I had left in earnest, understood as our common starting point, namely to the neo-Protestant, rational and revelatory."[204]

Brunner had represented a legitimate concern that he saw overlooked too quickly by Barth. The one-sidedness in Emil Brunner's anthropological problem found its mirror image counterpart in Barth's equally one-sided transfer of it and was thus almost provoked. Not everyone could leave such a grave theological problem as that of Christian anthropology untouched for twenty-five years like Barth.[205] However, two and a half decades later, Barth openly acknowledged the one-sidedness of the position he had then claimed and retrospectively confirmed the fundamental right (not the implementation!) of Brunner's concern.[206]

---

202. Brunner, *Natur und Gnade*, 10–11, 18–19, 40–41.

203. Brunner, *Natur und Gnade*, 6.

204. K. Barth, "Abschied," 33.

205. Barth presented his own anthropology, with its Christocentric approaches, in a more comprehensive form in 3.2 of his *Kirkliche Dogmatik* (1948).

206. See K. Barth, *Menschlichkeit Gottes*, 7.

THIRD PART

Brunner's View of Modern Natural Theology

3.1. PREMISE OF THOUGHT

According to Brunner, the "natural-theological view" is an immediate consequence of the misrecognition of the contrast between general and special revelation, as already described. In the following, Brunner's understanding of the real human being, its prerequisites, and the "doctrine of the starting point" peculiar to Brunner, which later provides the background for Barth's solution to the problem of natural theology, will be presented. According to Barth, the fundamental error of natural theology is to equate the relationship of nature to God with that of every human being to general revelation. However, Brunner was concerned with the use of this possible bridge to establish the relationship that God has sovereignly established with living humans. This relationship is not only sustained by God, who encounters humans, but also by the factually existing human beings as receivers of revelation. In the case of Jesus, however, he is a human being whose power in general revelation is particularly great, perhaps greater than that of all previous human beings. Therefore, Jesus is considered a religious "primus inter pares."[1]

---

1. See Ernst Troeltsch, "Offenbarung," 4:920; cited in Brunner, *Mittler*, 48.

Just as a shepherd seeks out a lost sheep until he finds it at the place of its wandering, the history of Jesus is an effort for humanity. The story of Jesus has a single incomprehensible meaning,[2] a meaning that the apostles certainly did not believe they were betraying the cause of the gospel in their pursuit of it,[3] and in whose pursuit, theology was eventually able to confidently follow its path.[4] The life of Jesus, historically reconstructed, can be placed in the contingency of worldly human history. This allows for a neutral, relative, but for Brunner, an unbelieving evaluation of the human Jesus. According to Brunner, Paul himself wrote the program for a proper eristic theology.

"For the weapons of our warfare are not carnal, but mighty through God to the pulling down of strongholds, casting down arguments" and "bringing every thought into captivity to the obedience of Christ."[5] Furthermore, Brunner strongly opposes the attitude of theological exclusivity that places revelation in an exclusive relationship to the reason and knowledge of the "natural" person, and notoriously rejects any connection through conscious engagement with the questions of the time, as well as any programmatic confrontation with the self- and world view of the unbeliever. For although revelation creates "a new understanding," it does not do so without taking natural understanding into account.[6] For Brunner, this is equivalent to unbelief, "because one cannot believe in a human being any more than one can see a sound or grasp a thought with one's hands."[7]

"For Brunner, engaging with revelation is merely 'stepping through human, humane possibilities.'"[8] If faith is an act of knowl-

---

2. See Brunner, *Offenbarung und Vernunft*, 409.

3. See 1 Cor 9:20–23.

4. Brunner, *Offenbarung und Vernunft*, 15.

5. See 2 Cor 10:4–5; see also all three vols. of Brunner, *Dogmatik*; here *christliche Lehre von Gott*, 19.

6. Brunner, *christliche Lehre von Gott*, 15–16; see Brunner, *Gebot und die Ordnungen*, 75.

7. See Brunner, *Mittler*. For reflection on faith in Christ, *Mittler*, 51.

8. Brunner, *Mittler*, 52.

edge, then it necessarily presupposes a relationship to reason. Brunner's concern with natural theology is for a theology in which true reason is even more evident in faith, and one that understands the divine message as an answer to the question of human existence in its being—in contradiction to it.[9]

The question of systematic method is addressed in terms of how this can be done rightly. The difference between the faithful and unbelieving consideration of revelation lies only in whether one stops at the fleshly reality of the word or perceives in it another, divine reality. It cannot be claimed that Brunner presents the essence of faith in a new and original way in terms of its positive content. Rather, the negative emphasis associated with it, which is undoubtedly strongly influenced by Barth, appears to be new. The real pathos of Brunner's entire argumentation repeatedly addresses the fact that a subjective factor in faith gains its own weight. Even titles given to Christ by modern theology,[10] such as "God's Word," "the true truth," do not change this if they only refer to Christ as "the primus inter pares," the climax of religious history.[11] For the renewal of the original word of creation in Jesus Christ leads to the Christological foundation of anthropology.[12] Human knowledge has its starting point in the word of God, which became flesh in Jesus Christ against sin.[13] From him comes the origin of humanity,[14] the sin or opposition,[15] the reality of humanity,[16] as well as the new, true humanity in view.[17] Therefore, subjective natural theology

---

9. See Brunner, *christliche Lehre von Kirche*, 251–52, 254–55.

10. Brunner is particularly referring here to the theologies of Schleiermacher and Ritschl.

11. Brunner, *Mediator*, 56.

12. See Brunner, "neue Barth," 97.

13. See Brunner, *Mystik und Wort*. The contrast between modern religious conceptions and Christian faith presented in Schleiermacher's theology, *Mystik und Wort*, 70.

14. Brunner, *Mystik und Wort*, 85ff.

15. Brunner, *Mystik und Wort*, 116ff.

16. Brunner, *Mystik und Wort*, 293ff.

17. Brunner, *Mystik und Wort*, 471ff.

has no practical value, because it is "rendered unnecessary and ineffective by the better knowledge that we have in Christ."[18]

From the perspective of the correct, objective natural theology,[19] the "subjective natural knowledge of God" becomes transparent and understandable in its essential core. Thus, it allows a view of the starting point, of what remains constant in the turning point from sin to faith, and illuminates the methodical approach of connection. As Brunner sarcastically remarks, natural theology is "old wineskins with new wine, which is offered as old."[20] He includes Schleiermacher's concept of the archetype, which typifies his anthropology, as the perfect humanity given by God, which could be reached through constant approximation.[21] Nevertheless, for Brunner, modern man resembles the lost son who has separated himself from his father in the desire for autonomy, but has fallen into contradiction with himself and into misery.[22]

The concept of "Urbild" in Schleiermacher's theology means an ideal image that the religious person can achieve through a divine creation. Thus, the concept of "Urbild" can be transformed from the concept of a general religion to that of a mediating faith.[23]

Brunner sees the faith in Christ abandoned when it is considered as an archetype of piety. Therefore, because of the contradiction in Schleiermacher's concept of archetype, Brunner calls for a certain disengagement from the empirical method of theology. This is a critique against the Cartesian concept of causality and its idea that one can come from the psychological, subjective, religious experiences to their cause, to God.[24] In his "second letter" to Sack, Schleiermacher famously asked the question:

---

18. See Brunner, *Natur und Gnade*, 193.
19. Brunner, *Natur und Gnade*, 207.
20. Brunner, *Mediator*, 56.
21. Brunner, *Mediator*, 67.
22. Brunner, *Mystik und Wort*, 473.
23. See Schleiermacher, *christliche Glaube*, 89, 100; also see Brunner, *Mediator*, 68.
24. See Jalkanen, *1909–1924*, 24–25.

Should the knot of history unravel in such a way that Christianity falls with barbarism and science with unbelief?[25]

It is a common feature of all shades of Schleiermacher's theology to reject this dilemma and opt for dualism. Brunner therefore considers Schleiermacher's talk of an ideal image unnecessary, as there can be no archetype that makes an image identical. Since Schleiermacher ignores the question of truth and the proper religious method, his view is vulnerable to the accusation of illusion.[26] Brunner, an intellectually minded seeker of religious truth, noticed the conflict between logical truth and irrational, psychological experience, which gave him the impetus for criticism.[27]

According to Brunner, there isn't "much difference" with Ritschl.[28] Ritschl viewed morality as latent religion since the moral person becomes religious because of their morality. The starting point of his thinking is the fundamental causal significance of morality for the moral conflict inherent in humans.[29] However, Ritschl simply replaced Schleiermacher's mystical concept of religion with the formulations of the rational-ethical worldview.[30] Wherever the supreme principle of this idealism, the idea of perfect love, is recognized and practically applied, be it by faith or the community, there is divinity for Ritschl. Theology exists in the tension between two poles: the divine message and the human situation. Its task is therefore determined on the one hand as "the self-reflection of the Christian community on the foundation, meaning and content of the message given and entrusted to it,"[31] and on the other hand as the confrontation of this message with the contemporary situation.

25. See Schleiermacher, " Über seine Glaubenslehre," esp. 146.
26. See Salakka, *Person und Offenbarung*, 35.
27. See Ernst Troeltsch, *Psychologie und Erkenntnistheorie*, 396.
28. Brunner, *Mediator*, 70.
29. See Brunner, *Grenzen der Humanität*; and *Anfänge der dialektischen Theologie* 1:269: "Only in this distress does the prospect of the wholly other open up, in which our redemption is assured."
30. Brunner, *Mediator*, 70.
31. Brunner, *christliche Lehre von Gott*, ix.

THIRD PART

Thus, moral consciousness also has a kind of pedagogical or mediating role here, but not in such a way that it itself brings about the transition to that "completely different" realm.[32]

Brunner finds Ritschl inconsistent in that he remains in independent religious knowledge but uses the principles of ethics as criteria: "However, there are theologians who adhere to such independent religious truth, but still derive their criteria from outside, namely from ethics, like Ritschl."[33]

According to Ritschl, the divinity of Jesus results a posteriori from the moral achievement of Jesus, which Brunner disappointingly notes with respect to modern natural theology. However, for Brunner, the debate with modern theology is not over yet.

3.2. THE POSSIBILITY OF AN UNBROKEN CONNECTION BETWEEN GOD AND HUMANITY AS A ROOT OF THE CONCEPT OF REVELATION

According to modern thinking, human reason can explain the world as a world from within itself, guided by a single principle, reason. Thus, reason identifies itself as the creator of this principle.[34] To find God, the rational human being essentially only needs to listen to themselves and their reason.[35] Brunner sees in the modern world a common point where both the human way and God's way, and accordingly also revelation and reason, converge and "almost become one, only to then move apart all the more vehemently."[36]

The Christian-medieval world placed the human being and their reason under the command and claim of a transcendent God.[37] The basic model of methodological and substantive discus-

---

32. See K. Barth, "Christian in Society," 1:5–6.
33. See Brunner, *Symbolische*, 5.
34. Brunner, *Mediator*, 82.
35. Brunner, *Mediator*, 84.
36. See Brunner, "Gesetz und Offenbarung," 1:290.
37. Brunner, *Mediator*, 82.

sions on the question of anthropology, which recurs like a theme with variations in Brunner's later works, as well as individual new theoretical elements, point even further back to the pre-critical early period.[38] Based on this foundation, Brunner strives to deepen and refine this model of thought and its supporting concepts. Here, human reason has become the subject of a pronounced theological interest as a counterpart to the revelation event; thus, the theologian must "know every point precisely where human reason offers God the summit, as he wants to make clear how revelation affects the natural human being."[39]

According to Brunner, bringing this awareness to light can happen according to some principles of reason. The first step is that of thinking compared to the intuitive introduction method, which Brunner criticizes in his early writing "The Misery of Theology."[40] This already clearly indicates the beginning of the confrontation with irrationalism. The second, according to Brunner, is the path of "meditative abstraction" founded by Schleiermacher, which "feels and sees God himself as the innermost core, as the center of human-natural existence"—here, feeling and mysticism have received their proper place.[41] Brunner explicitly emphasizes that omitting them would mean agnosticism and would destroy mysticism.[42] The third path is that of moral volition. According to Brunner, these views are found "in the ethical sense when the highest goal is seen in the theoretical activity of humans: bios theoretikos."[43]

The moral person therefore appears as a participant in this idea and thus as a small god. He corresponds most to the

38. See Brunner, "Gesetz und Offenbarung."
39. Brunner, ""Gesetz und Offenbarung, 290.
40. See Brunner, "Elend der Theologie," 50–51
41. Brunner, *Mediator*, 86.
42. Brunner, *Symbolische*, 51: "The complete elimination of immanence is identical with agnosticism"; see also Brunner, *Symbolische*, 15; see Gyllenberg, *Reunamuistutuksia barthilaiseen teologiaan*, 56ff, 99ff: "We do believe, however, that we do not contradict the facts of religious history if we designate mysticism as the heart of religion."
43. Brunner, *Symbolische*, 126ff.

self-confidence of modern man: "Man is good."[44] According to Kant, this imperative, the categorical imperative, which arises from the moral reasoning of man, should be fulfilled by man.[45] In the logical development of his thoughts on the consciousness of morality and autonomy, Kant consistently speaks of an "idea of radical evil"[46] that asserts itself in man and is in sharp contradiction to his practical reason based on moral autonomy. Although Kant insists on the coherence of his categorical imperative and moral autonomy, his moral idealism is vehemently rejected by the reformers because it directly contradicts the justitia aliena, the righteousness given by Christ in faith.[47] An imperative that cannot be fulfilled due to the constitution of the one to whom it is addressed is unreasonable. Faith acknowledges practical reason in its office and the law in its severity, and indeed presupposes this critical recognition of the boundary, the recognition of evil.[48] According to Brunner, no bridge can be built from Kant's moral reasoning to Christian faith.[49]

The fourth way, according to Brunner, is that of historicism. However, Brunner sees in the idea of immanent evolution a source of consequential errors that led to theological fallacies, such as those concerning research findings on the continuity of human existence with the Absolute.[50] Hegel's philosophy of history, according to Brunner, describes the gradual "overcoming of the relative opposition between existence and the divine."[51]

---

44. Brunner, *Mediator*, 87.

45. See Brunner, *Mediator*, 87.

46. Brunner, *Mediator*, 90: Brunner notes that Kant had consistently carried this idea further, "shattering the entire modern foundation of Kantian thinking."

47. Brunner, *Mediator*, 91.

48. Brunner, *Grenzen der Humanität*, 1:271; see Brunner, "Offenbarung als Grund," 1:317.

49. See Stange, *Christianity and Modern Worldview*, 37, 40.

50. Brunner, *Mediator*, 92.

51. Brunner, *Mediator*, 92: In his philosophy of history, Hegel understands history as the final phase of the triadic dialectic, as God's coming-to-self through the spiritualization of matter.

History, according to Hegel, does not need a mediation outside of its own self-movement to God, no God-man mediator.[52] However, Brunner shows with the dialectical method, corresponding categorical differentiation between biblical and historical truth. Truth happens timelessly in historical uniqueness, according to Brunner. The word of revelation as truth is the only and sufficient source of all truth, reason, and history.[53] However, as Brunner points out, faith in its continuity could have been shaken by war and various global crises, as well as philosophical doctrines, in recent times. Does this pave the way to faith? In a paradoxical sense, it must be said that human beings are beings that exist in contradiction between creation and sin, god-related and godless, always holding God responsible and denying their responsibility.

3.3. DAS NEUE MENSCHENVERSTÄNDNIS IN WAHRHEIT ALS BEGEGNUNG

3.3.1. The Human Being in the Contradiction of Creation and Sin

In 1937, there was a clear turning point in Brunner's thinking. He presented a deliberately anti-idealist anthropology in his work *Man in Revolt*.[54] Christian knowledge of man is determined by two basic ideas, namely that man is created in the image of God and that he is a sinner. Therefore, the Christian doctrine of man is threefold:

> Doctrine of Origin, Doctrine of Opposition, and Doctrine of the Reality of Man in the Contradiction of Origin and Opposition.[55]

Sin is the contradiction of the whole against the whole within the whole. Therefore, in all human aspects, the sinner is doubly determined, in contradiction to himself. In the sinner, there is

---

52. Brunner, *Mediator*, 92.
53. Brunner, *Offenbarung und Vernunft*, 373.
54. See also Brunner, *christliche Lehre von Schöpfung*, 57–145.
55. Brunner, *Man in Revolt*, 72.

nothing that is still in the image of God, which is not also surrounded by sins, and there is no sinful act that would not still be a testimony to the God-likeness as personal.[56] This results in the fact that man is a "man in contradiction"; he is the existing one in contradiction to his own original, created being. The dubiousness of human existence, all confusion, all disintegration, emanate from the responsible act of the spirit, they have their origin in sin:

> The true mystery of man is the contradiction in his essence, not the composite nature of his body and soul; not that he is both a part of the world and more than the world, but that the original unity of all these elements has been lost, and that they have become opposed to each other instead of cooperating and working for one another.[57]

Sin is the key to understanding human existence. Understood in its radicality, it documents the godlessness of man outside of Christ. The natural man, the rational man, the religious man, cannot at any moment overcome his factual separation from God, even if he tends to trivialize or ignore it. His existence as such is a contradiction to God, is remoteness from God, is separation from the origin. No way leads back to God, but the movement, from which he himself is seized, is that of departure.[58]

Anyone who thinks otherwise has not yet understood the importance of sin. Here, in the doctrine of man created for God in the state of corruption, theological anthropology has its legitimate

---

56. Brunner, *Man in Revolt*, 72, 77, 166: "The true core of Christian doctrine . . . is the understanding of man in the contradiction of creation-origin and its opposite, sin"; see also *Man in Revolt*, 186: "Therefore, there is nothing human that does not suggest the original Imago Dei, and there is nothing human that does not indicate the perversity of human nature."

"The contradiction we are talking about is the coexistence of the divine creative determination and its opposite in the sinful self-determination of man. Thus, not the truism that everyone is 'not a well-wrought book,' but a human being with his contradiction', not the fact of a lower and a higher self', the two souls', oh, in my breast, but this specific contradiction of creation-origin and sin is presupposed here."

57. Brunner, *Man in Revolt*, 164.
58. Brunner, *Mediator*, 98–128, 311.

place. The solution to the mystery of man is contained in the two concepts of creation and sin. Brunner outlines an anthropological program in the following three lines of thought: doctrine of origin, doctrine of opposition, and doctrine of the reality of man. He understands the fall into sin as an expression of the primal opposition:[59] that man, who has his foundation in God, does not assert himself against him out of defiance and rebellion, but in the perception of a possibility that results from the image of God. The bad conscience, isolation, and actual sins point to this. Origin and opposition are united only in man as a contradiction. Nevertheless, man does not stop "being in God's word."[60] This provokes the inner contradiction in man, which manifests itself in external contradictions (the constant revolution of man against God is effectively shown in the revolutions of this world). Based on these contradictions, Brunner judges with the utmost decisiveness all attempts at autonomy by man: idealism, false humanism, and autonomous human striving are listed among the precautions (and only in some cases does Brunner weigh up the pros and cons, as Barth did when he emphasized them).

The sin affects the overall reality of the human and his world by causing a division between the true and real human, and between truth and reality in general. This idea is so important to Brunner's understanding of the sinner that he even writes it in the subtitle of his anthropology: "The human in contradiction. The Christian teaching of the true and real human." This position regarding the contradictions characterizes Brunner's dialectical key position. His theology has consistently and fundamentally revealed itself as a dialectical theology from its innermost approach and concern. In attempting to understand Brunner from his own theological perspective, his dogmatics are by no means a mediating theology, but rather a position asserted between the extremes of the Right and the Left. We cannot summarize here Brunner's

---

59. Brunner, *Man in Revolt*, 121.
60. Brunner, *Man in Revolt*, 165.

view of identifying his middle position between the two theological camps characterized by Barth and Bultmann.[61]

The justification for the paradoxical-dialectical character lies on the one hand, in the fact that in his revelation, God is primarily subject and not object.[62] Revelation is God's self-communication, a personal relationship, truth, and encounter. However, all-natural rational knowledge of truth is essentially object-knowledge based on the object-subject schema. This essential opposition between revelation and rational truth constitutes Brunner's first dialectic. It exists in relation to the knowledge of divine revelation in that "the same reason that is always a prerequisite on its formal side is always determined, on its material side . . . as sin, in opposition to the Word of God."[63]

The second dialectic arises from the question of evaluating the relationship between reason distorted by sin and revelation.

> Sin does not prevent humans from recognizing and understanding things of the world, natural laws, natural facts, and human beings in their natural, historical, and cultural manifestations. However, the more it concerns the innermost being of humans, their position towards God, the more the sinful delusion proves to be effective. Therefore, the maximum of sinful delusion can be found in the knowledge of God himself.[64]

So, in the knowledge that true and false are mixed in the recognition of the sinful person, a third dialectic emerges from this interplay of moments of truth and precaution. The relationship between moments of truth and precautions is based on the fundamental determination of human existence as being in contradiction. However, Brunner's third declension must not be misunderstood as a quantitative relationship in any case. It is a dialectical relationship because it is not a natural but a spiritual

---

61. Brunner, *christliche Lehre von Kirche*, 9, 247, 249; also *christliche Lehre von Gott*, 378.
62. See Brunner, "Theologie und Kirche," 417.
63. Brunner, *Man in Revolt*, 552.
64. Brunner, *christliche Lehre von Schöpfung*, 34.

relationship, namely a contradiction.⁶⁵ Although, as shown above, we cannot talk about "a directly ascertainable continuity between nature and grace, reason and revelation" with Barth in view of the entirety of Brunner's methodology and its implementation, the entry point for a natural theology is threatened to lie here.⁶⁶ Thus, the theological discourse is simultaneously broken in three ways with reason, which is the dialectic of Brunner's method. From the dialectical relationship between God and man, the intra-anthropological dialectic of man in contradiction, man in opposition of God—likeness and being a sinner, emerged.

3.3.2. The Restoration of Imago Dei as an "Everlasting Revelation Event"

The question of connection leads right into Brunner's anthropology, into his doctrine of "man in contradiction." M. Kähler sees in the human disposition for religion and morality, in the awareness of God, in the consciousness of responsibility (conscience), and in the consciousness of guilt the decisive internal prerequisites, the connections or points of contact that allow for believing understanding.⁶⁷ The fact that man exists "in contradiction" means that the address of God also affects him in contradiction, in connection and opposition; that it addresses and burdens him with his original responsibility just as much as it holds him accountable for his factual irresponsibility, so that what formally serves as a "point of connection for the Gospel" is at the same time materially "the point of highest opposition and rejection."⁶⁸

Since Barth has taken up the topic of connection rather pragmatically, the idea of a point of connection cannot be valid according to him. Regarding the missionary—the most popular example when it comes to connection—Barth says:

65. See Brunner, *Offenbarung und Vernunft*, 75.

66. Brunner, *Offenbarung und Vernunft*, 75. See also Barth's response to Brunner, "Nein!"

67. See Kähler, *Science of Christian Doctrine*, §76.5, 80ff.

68. Brunner, *Man in Revolt*, 531.

He will connect . . . all language is a connection!—to the entire reason, why not also to the religious life of his listeners, but he will not enrich the Christian confession and the Christian sermon through the teaching of a point of connection of a natural revelation before revelation.[69]

If connection is still to be talked about here, it can only be understood in a dialectical sense. Brunner never wanted to teach anything other than such a dialectical connection; according to his own words, it remained the "constant center of his theological thinking."[70] If the dialectical relationship between connection and opposition is to be more precisely defined, Brunner's own distinction between formal and material personality, his doctrine of the Imago, must be referred to.[71] "The Imago of man, on its formal side, as the form, as the structure of responsible human being, is just as generally presupposed as it is irretrievably lost on its material side, as the content of human being, as responsible being-in-love."[72] But love is the reality. Truly human being is not creative, but responsible:

> But this has been revealed and given to us not on the Acropolis, but on Golgotha, where God revealed His and our truth as love.[73]

The New Testament references to the imago Dei renewed in Jesus Christ presuppose that "structural Godlikeness" already, they look to the "material filling of this structure" and urge for the

---

69. See K. Barth, "Theologie und die Mission," 214.

70. Brunner, *Man in Revolt*, 531; also see Brunner, "Gesetz und Offenbarung," col. 53ff.; 1:290ff.

71. Brunner, *Man in Revolt*, 20.

72. Brunner, *Man in Revolt*, 166; "Here the responsibility is given, and here biblical understanding is finally separated from idealistic understanding—not first task, but gift; not first demand, but life; not law, but grace. The word that calls upon the human being to respond is not a 'Thou shalt', but a 'Thou mayest be'. The original word is not an imperative, but the indicative of divine love: 'Thou art mine'" (Brunner, *Man in Revolt*, 100).

73. Brunner, *Man in Revolt*, 70.

response of reverent and grateful love that would truly correspond to God's own gift of love.[74]

In the face of Jesus Christ, Brunner summarizes his view in the following sentences:

> We are created as spiritual-physical persons whose personhood is based on their responsibility, and whose responsibility is grounded in God's call. This call of God, however, is to be understood from Jesus Christ not as a mere categorical imperative or as a moral law, but as the call of God to communion with Him, the Creator, and through Him to communion with humanity.[75]

Although Brunner has abandoned the term of a formal Imago that he used in his earlier writings, he "cannot avoid distinguishing between a formal structure and a material filling of the Imago Dei."[76] The formal structure is indicated by the Old Testament term, which refers to the "responsive actuality that constitutes the essence of every human being," the enduring subjectivity, the ability to hear and speak, responsible freedom, which distinguishes us from the animal world. Barth and Brunner have separated over the question of the point of contact and thus also over a "formal Imago."[77] Barth sees the personality of the human being also regarding its formal structure, revealed only in the revelation of Christ, and recognizes the imago Dei of the human being only in the image of the God-human. Brunner can agree with him only to the extent that it concerns the understanding of what is meant by the imago Dei and responsible personal being. However, that the revelation is indisputably to be regarded as the only basis for the recognition of responsible personal being does not mean that it is identical with personal being.

Barth's objection therefore results from an incorrect identification of the *ratio cognoscendi* with the *ratio essendi*. Rather,

74. Brunner, *christliche Lehre von Schöpfung*, 67–73.
75. Brunner, *christliche Lehre von Schöpfung*, 86.
76. Brunner, *Man in Revolt*, 499; see also Gestrich, *Neuzeitliches Denken*, 72–206; also see Brunner, *Natur und Gnade*.
77. The same, 27–72, 172–206.

the ground of being of human beings is the creative word of God, in which humanity has its basis and origin. All theology is since "there is a relationship of similarity between God's speaking and the human, between God's personhood and the human, and therefore between God's being and creaturely being."[78]

Brunner's view on the lack of relationality in revelation differs primarily from Barth's, according to whom the revelation of God is presuppositionless, not only in terms of cognitive but also existential relationship. Concerning the sinful human being, it applies that wherever he knows the truth, he does so in a false way, that his sense is distorted into contradiction, that even his correct insights are misguided and misapplied, that he denies the responsibility entrusted to him, in short, that "the human being of the sinner is a corrupted human being."[79] However, this perversion does not mean the annulment and eradication of his reason: "Man is not assumed or made a tabula rasa by the Word of God."[80] Although "the present humanitas . . . is not, as Catholicism teaches, the right original human nature," it is also not "a theologically irrelevant profane fact," as Barth teaches."[81]

Even though humanity is corrupted and perverted, *humanitas* is an undeniable fact, without which the sinner would not be addressed as a human being at all. It seems equally unconvincing, in line with Barth, to understand the "image of God" as the basic form of humanity or to see the image of God in the freedom of human behavior towards the world and its "own reality."[82] Brunner refers to the Incarnation of God as the "foundation of the knowledge of the Imago Dei of man in its truth and depth," "the Imago Dei of man in its indestructibility on the formal side, but at the same time the objective possibility for the divine revelation in his

---

78. Brunner, *christliche Lehre von Schöpfung*, 29–30; also see Brunner, "neue Barth," 90, 92.
79. Brunner, *Man in Revolt*, 531.
80. Brunner, *Man in Revolt*, 550.
81. Brunner, *Man in Revolt*, 531.
82. So Moltmann, "Mensch," 157–58.

Word."[83] However, this insight can only be precisely formulated with the help of dialogical personalism.[84]

3.4. THE TRUE PERSONAL ENCOUNTER

In 1938, Brunner published the smallest work in comparison to his other works, but perhaps the most significant in terms of its content, *Truth as Encounter: Six Lectures on Christian Understanding of Truth*, which offers the easiest access to understanding his theology. There, Brunner demonstrates that in the Bible there is neither subjective nor objective truth, and that truth, in the biblical sense, is not a rational concept in the realm of subject-object opposition; rather, Person-Truth refers to an event: an encounter between God and humans. "This biblical truth is as different from what is otherwise called truth as this personal encounter . . . is different from the confessional grasp of a fact."[85]

At the same time, the argument is made that "the use of the subject-object opposition in the relationship of faith truth . . . represents a disastrous misunderstanding. Biblical understanding of truth cannot be grasped by the subject-object opposition but is distorted by it."[86] The relationship between faith and God's Word is not an intellectual relationship between subject and object, but a relationship of true personal encounter. However, since every personal encounter, as a matter of its spiritual nature, occurs in speaking and being spoken to, in word and answer, the event of God's self-revelation possesses both a word and an address character. The word of God is "confrontational speech." Address, or more precisely, claim, that demands an appropriate answer and thus makes the human being responsible.[87] For this, any seemingly

---

83. Brunner, *Natur und Gnade*, 42: Brunner understands "Word" (in quotation marks) to mean Jesus Christ, who is more than just a word.
84. Brunner, *Man in Revolt*, 497–98.
85. See Brunner, *Wahrheit als Begegnung*, 57.
86. Brunner, *Wahrheit als Begegnung*, 14.
87. Brunner, *Mystik und Wort*, 159; see *christliche Lehre von Kirche*, 473; also 293: "One must understand responsibility literally . . . : as being called to account, as having to answer or give an account."

historical aspect must be radically demythologized, which also concerns Adam's state before the fall and the so-called original sin. Only a radical "abandonment of Adam's history" enables a "consistent implementation of the strictly theological, because strictly actualistic personalistic Imago concept," according to Brunner.

This insight is anticipated by Martin Kähler.[88] In his work *God and Man*, Brunner explained the following: since humans can only recognize God as someone with whom they have a personal encounter, and the place of personal encounter for humans is history, God reveals himself, according to human knowledge, "in a real, historical you, in a person."[89] God encountered humanity through Jesus "in historical reality . . . therefore, anyone who plays with the non-existence of the historical Jesus is playing with the abolition of Christian truth, just as much as anyone who expected the repetition" of a Christian revelation of God:[90] for faith, it remains entirely irrelevant in which historical contexts Christ existed. Because "for faith, the what and the that are everything; the when, how, and why are indifferent. But not only is faith indifferent to history as such, it also stands in sharp and conscious opposition to historical thinking."[91] Naive ideas in this regard are associated with the pre-Copernican "spacetime image," and only the transcendental distinction between creation and sin remains, which must, however, be interpreted strictly in a Christocentric way.[92]

---

88. Brunner, *Mensch im Widerspruch*, 114, 497–98.
89. See Brunner, *Gott und Mensch*, 21.
90. See Brunner, "Christusbotschaft im Kampf," especially 8–9.
91. See Brunner, *Erlebnis, Erkenntnis und Glaube*, 105; also see *Mystik und Wort*, 220, 226, 434. Brunner, *Mensch im Widerspruch*, 88–91, 382–400; see also *christliche Lehre von Schöpfung*, 59–63.
92. See Brunner, "andere Aufgabe," 255.

CONCLUSION

Results and Outlook

EMIL BRUNNER AND KARL BARTH share the approach of a radical theology of revelation. Theology's dogmatic task is to repeatedly "call the church to reflect on the given word of God."[1] The addressee of the word of God is human beings. Therefore, theology has another task that is no less important: to consider the relationship between the word of God on the one hand and human beings on the other, and to attempt to explain the conditions and possibilities of understanding the word of God. Brunner refers to this task as Eristic. He emphasizes the one-sided moment of the dispute, while Eristic also expresses the dialogical aspect of the argument.[2] Therefore, Eristic means connection. The younger Barth would have probably agreed with this, but in a confrontation with Barth, to which Brunner felt compelled due to the changed question (nature and grace), Brunner assigned a task to Eristic that is distinct from the dogmatic task.

In his book *Man in Revolt*, Brunner further clarifies his view of humanity by more explicitly grounding human absurdity, rationality, and decision-making theologically, even Christological: For Brunner's understanding of humanity, his distinction between "formal" and "material" imago Dei is fundamental. As a creature of God, humanity is essentially determined by its being in the image

---

1. See Leipold, *Missionarische Theologie*, 127.
2. See Brunner, *Mensch im Widerspruch*, 97.

CONCLUSION

of God. Brunner describes this as the human's subjectivity. This Christian humanity is about responsibility in community, being eloquent towards God, and being related to the human "thou."[3] According to Brunner, Ferdinand Ebner, Friedrich Gogarten, and Martin Buber were pioneers in the development of a new position that moved beyond both subjective religious experiences and dogmatic objectivism, a position that went beyond Barth as well, as he also explains autobiographically.

The formal imago Dei is the epitome of this dignity, which cannot be destroyed by sin. If the formal imago Dei persists despite the loss of the material, that is to say, if the contradictory human being can still be addressed, then a formal starting point is given for the redemptive message of the gospel. The human's sense of truth and beauty, creative ability, moral consciousness, fear and longing, doubt and hope, awareness of the holy and religious, are all traces of the image of God. However, this is dialectically contrasted with the misery of humanity.[4]

Why does Brunner emphasize this "word power"? Barth, tellingly, speaks of "revelation power" and is therefore criticized by Brunner. The whole debate is essentially about whether, in addition to the revelation of Christ, there is still a general revelation and, if so, what significance it has. Above all, the laws of creation are somehow known to human beings.[5] Such an understanding of human beings implies an analogous understanding of creation. Luther's doctrine of the two kingdoms is affirmed. The human being who acts in accordance with the laws of creation and preservation, quite apart from their motives, does God's work. Despite all perversion and obscurity, the world as God's creation testifies to reality. Although such revelation in nature, history, or conscience may not be sufficient or may remain ambiguous, the double revelation of God in creation and in Christ is unquestionable.[6] However,

---

3. Brunner, *Mensch im Widerspruch*, 170ff., 178ff.
4. See Brunner, *Natur und Gnade*, 24ff.
5. Brunner, *Natur und Gnade*, 38.
6. See Brunner, *Natur und Gnade*, 177: "Where God does something, he imprints upon what he does the stamp of his nature. Therefore, the creation of

the relationship between both revelations must also be clearly determined.[7]

Brunner's theses provoked Barth's passionate "no." The intensity of his reaction was certainly influenced by the situation in 1934. Neither an eristic theology, which demonstrates the failure of unbelieving existence, nor a natural theology should become an independent topic in theology, even if it is only to negate it.[8] However, emphasizing the situation of the conflict in 1934 too much simplifies the opposition in a gross manner. Despite some misunderstandings, it is a substantive opposition. The particular emphasis on the undestroyed formal imago Dei raises suspicion in Barth, although Brunner does not deny it.

However, this sharp antithesis is not the endpoint of the debate, but rather a certain convergence occurs during the discussion. Is grace less grace because Brunner speaks of a certain knowledge of God that is accessible to humans through the law, through conscience? Barth is concerned about the solution of the so-called preservation grace of Christ, which, like the ordinances, has an independent dignity. Nevertheless, according to Brunner, in the abundance and excess of concrete life, human beings are dependent and open to God.[9] This is where the redemption of humanity is linked, nowhere else, not with their dialectical reasoning or moral will. "The abolition of the contradiction between the real and the true human being"[10] occurs solely in hearing the gospel, the

---

the world is also revelation, self-communication of God."

7. Approaches to a double understanding of revelation are already found in Brunner's Christology monograph *Mediator* (1927, 12–21). Later, in dealing with the philosophical question, he devoted a separate investigation to the problems arising from this for a Christian theory of knowledge in his monograph *Revelation and Reason* (1941).

8. See Brunner, *Mensch im Widerspruch*, 215–496.

9. Brunner, *Mensch im Widerspruch*, 497.

10. Brunner, *Mensch im Widerspruch*, 555: "Being-in-responsibility, being-in-decision, being-in-freedom, and all the determinations that depend further upon this basic determination, such as guilt, etc., are those that, although they are formal, are thought of quite differently from the Christian concept of creation than without it."

CONCLUSION

message of the crucified and risen Jesus Christ. If the human being hears this message, their contradictory being is contradicted, and their original connection to God is once again demanded by God.[11] Barth must strictly say "no" to the attempt to give weight to the question of the connection point, to designate it as one or the other, particularly urgent task of theology today.[12]

Brunner does not retract his thesis on the remaining formal imago Dei in humans. In his book, he extensively searches for traces of humanity and explicitly repeats that the personal structure is the very point of connection he seeks for proclamation. Brunner speaks of a certain, albeit corruptible, knowledge of God in fallen humans. He emphasizes that the same point, the actual point of connection, is also the point of greatest contrast. Despite all formal identity of humans, their material determination is attacked to the utmost in encountering the gospel by sin. Adding to this is Brunner's radical rejection of attempts to provide an existential-philosophical foundation for theology,[13] as he says, "The foundation and substance of theology is not an objectively existing highest being or essence, nor an inner human feeling or the like, but the relationship between God and human beings."[14] Of course, this relationship is not something that arises based on the relationship between two equal partners. Only because God is "a God towards humans" can humans experience themselves as "from God as humans."[15]

It could be that Brunner strictly distinguishes between a general Logos (*Logos asarkos*) and the incarnate Word, the historical Christ. When he says that human beings have their foundation of being in the Word of God, in the Logos, it could refer to this general Logos that had nothing directly to do with the name Jesus

---

11. Barth, "Nein!," 52: "The question of the 'starting point' then should not have occurred to Brunner in an anthropological context, but only in a Christological, pneumatological, ecclesiological context."
12. See Thuk 1931, 2.111–12: "Theology and Ontology."
13. See Brunner, *Wahrheit als Begegnung*, 91.
14. Brunner, *Wahrheit als Begegnung*, 96.
15. See Barth, *Kirchliche Dogmatik* III, 2, 157.

and the history he represents (so Barth's assumption[16]). One could understand why Brunner did not retract his earlier theses despite all criticism. This general Logos, for which Jesus Christ would only be the basis of knowledge, would likely allow for a "Christian natural theology" to be established here. "The Word of God is then only the word of a creator to be distinguished from the Lord of the covenant, and only from Him as such is it universally valid that human beings have their reality in it."[17]

Despite all the understanding between Barth and Brunner, one can hardly agree with Balthasar's assessment that peace has been made with Emil Brunner. Despite Barth's willingness to engage with Brunner's ideas, it is clear that this is a critical engagement. Deeper theological differences lie behind the problem of the starting point and natural theology. Ultimately, Barth's critical questions are always christological questions for Brunner. The most important question Barth raises concerns the being of humans in the Word of God. In answering this question, Brunner speaks about the Word.

> For the Word is the way in which Spirit communicates with Spirit, Subject with Subject, Will with Will. But it is not human words, but God's Word alone that is able to do so.[18]

As reported by Berger-Gebhardt, Brunner's life's work, as the *Church Times* suggests, may serve as a critical beacon for securing a better future amidst the crisis plaguing our world. His spiritual impact, whether knowingly or unknowingly assumed, continues to expand.[19]

Another important question is that of the concept of personhood: Brunner repeatedly emphasizes that the concept of personhood must be filled with Christology. Barth appeals to this against Brunner, now demanding such a positive filling in his statements

16. Barth, *Kirchliche Dogmatik* III, 2, 157.
17. Barth, *Kirchliche Dogmatik* III, 2, 103.
18. Barth, *Kirchliche Dogmatik* III, 2, 103.
19. See also Krause and Müller, *TRE*, 8:241.

CONCLUSION

about the personhood and decision-making ability of humans. In his criticism, he seems to even go beyond his earlier position. What Brunner says about this capacity for decision-making in humans is not determined enough for Barth.

It should not and cannot be about fully presenting Barth's position and delving into his theological approach in this context. Rather, it is precisely through Barth's critical questions that Brunner's position should be examined more closely. As we have shown, Brunner's theology was significantly shaped through his engagement with Barth. Understanding this debate is therefore of paramount importance in order to appropriately appreciate Brunner's work in its independence and its particular goals. Brunner not only formulated "the other task of theology" in general terms in relation to Barth, but he also specifically and comprehensively fulfilled this other task in his eristic and his ethics related to natural law and the laws of creation.

Although the revelation in creation only reveals its ultimate depth and truth through the revelation in Christ, humans are still bound by this knowledge of the general grace that is active in creation. God shows his grace to humans in his creation by establishing certain orders, "creation orders" such as marriage. His understanding of Christian truth as a truth of encounter also belongs in this context.

EPILOGUE

A Final Reflection on Emil Brunner and His Impact on Religious-Philosophical Method

THE SWISS CITY OF WINTERTHUR bore witness to the birth of Emil Brunner in 1889, a child who was destined to leave his imprint on the realms of theology and philosophy. His formative years found him traversing English-speaking nations, nurturing young minds as a high school teacher while assiduously pursuing his own scholarly journey. The humble town of Obstalden was the backdrop to his pastoral debut, and his first written exploration, a piece titled "Experience, Knowledge, and Faith," served as his initiation into the dialectical theology movement. As a dear confidant of Karl Barth, Brunner found himself at the heart of this nascent movement.

The year 1924 witnessed Brunner's ascension to the position of professor of systematic theology in Zurich. His sermons at the Zurich Frauenmünster attracted an eclectic congregation, resonating deeply with their spiritual quest. His prolific pen gave birth to seminal works such as *Mysticism and the Word*, *The Mediator*, *Philosophy of Religion in Protestant Theology*, and *The Commandment and the Orders*, to name but a few. Yet, his life was tinged with personal tragedy—the loss of two sons. Despite these tragic setbacks, Brunner continued his ecumenical mission in Japan before his death in Zurich in 1966.

EPILOGUE

Brunner's stance within the dialectical theology movement was a study in distinction. Along with Barth and Bultmann, he championed the radical revelation theology approach, placing Christ at the center and dismissing religion and autonomous philosophy as mere human constructs. However, Brunner's interpretation of these principles set him apart from his contemporaries. His impassioned critique of mysticism and idealism underscored humanity's original sin—the quest for autonomy. According to Brunner, this pursuit engenders a conflict between reason and revelation, as humanity's yearning for autonomy stands in stark contradiction to obedience to God.

The echoes of Kierkegaard's philosophy reverberate in Brunner's work. He integrated Kierkegaard's thought into dialectical theology more than any other figure in the movement. Despite his critiques, Brunner was not entirely dismissive of philosophy. Rather, he envisioned a Christian philosophy anchored in obedient reason.

In response to the secularization sweeping across European societies, Brunner embarked on a quest to revive a pertinent natural theology. His aim was to ensure that theological teachings resonated with the unchurched, specifically nonbelievers, intellectuals, and the young. He invoked various biblical passages, such as Rom 1:18–20 and 2:14–15, to substantiate the legitimacy of natural theology. His argument posited that God's revelation in creation precedes his revelation in reconciliation through Christ. However, Brunner acknowledged that humanity distorts this creation revelation, crafting their own godly images, thereby making their disobedience indefensible.

According to Brunner, the objective aspect of God's natural revelation corresponds to humanity's subjective likeness to God. He interpreted this likeness as a formal receptiveness, the ability to comprehend God's Word. Yet, such understanding is contingent upon God's self-revelation. In Brunner's theology, the "point of connection" lies in the human capacity for formal receptiveness, but it is only through God's Word that humans can truly hear and believe.

EPILOGUE

This position elicited a polemical retort from Barth in his work "No!" (1934). Barth sought to deconstruct Brunner's distinction between material and formal, arguing that even the formally understood likeness to God already possesses material content. Barth insisted that it is God's Word itself that establishes the point of connection. He labeled Brunner's theology as "mediating theology" and perceived this compromising approach as the misfortune of the German Evangelical Church in its struggles.

Aligning himself with figures such as Paul Althaus, Werner Elert, and Walter Künneth, Brunner proposed an order-theological concept, instituting a double distinction between the will of the Creator and the Redeemer, and between law and commandment. Brunner posited that God's will initially confronts us as law, transforming into a commandment solely through the lens of faith. This law, embodying God's will, demands recognition and consideration from all, thereby manifesting as accessible to all people. The idea of orders of creation is inseparable from Brunner's personalistic anthropology, where he conceives the human essence as self-responsibility towards others, only genuinely discernible through the prism of love. Post-fall, human existence, devoid of love, has resulted in the inability to fulfill its responsibility towards the neighbor, giving rise to opposition instead of community.

Nonetheless, Brunner acknowledged the possibility of community in the face of unbelief, a reality mirrored in everyday life. He deciphered this paradox through his concept of the orders of creation. Despite the inability to recognize and enforce the commandment due to unbelief, the law can still find recognition and enforcement. In the absence of communities founded in love, there exist those founded by law, referred to by Brunner as the orders of creation.

For Brunner, the orders of creation are the "unchangeable prerequisites" of human coexistence underpinning all historical life, with their form mutable but their basic structure unwavering. They guide humans towards one another and bind them in a specific way. These orders include marriage and family, communities

EPILOGUE

driven by the quest for sustenance and livelihood, national and legal communities, and the church as a visible entity.

As we navigate the labyrinth of Emil Brunner's religious-philosophical method and his take on natural theology, we are struck by the indelible mark his thought has left on the dialectical theology movement. His unique lens on these concepts continues to shape theological discourse, catalyzing an ongoing dialogue and examination among scholars today.

Brunner's oeuvre stands as a testament to his profound understanding of the intricate interplay between faith, philosophy, and the human condition. A significant aspect of his theology is his perspective on the state, which he perceives as a legal and power order contradicting God's good creative will. From Brunner's perspective, it's only in relation to sin that the state can gain positive significance, serving to maintain natural communities through legal coercion in our fallen world. Thus, the state, even in its imperfect form, points to the good will of God behind the orders of creation.

Contrary to the state, Brunner sees the orders of creation as emanating from God's positive creative will, not rooted in sin. However, this only applies to their prehistorical structure, not their historical manifestations, which are marred by the reality of sin. Despite this brokenness, the orders of creation, including the state, serve as a divine arrangement compelling fundamentally community-less humans to form communities.

A dialectic emerges in Brunner's theology between the orders of creation (law) and redemption (commandment). As the Creator, God demands recognition and integration into his orders. Simultaneously, as the Redeemer, he demands the non-recognition of the sinful form of these orders and a new action in view of the coming kingdom of God. This dialectic interweaves acceptance and refusal, conservative and revolutionary attitudes.

However, Brunner's positioning of social institutions as orders of creation invites critique. This perspective lends a conservative tendency and an emphasis on preservation that can inhibit a radical critique of these institutions. While the orders of creation serve to ward off evil, they can be seen to carry a divine dignity that is difficult to reconcile with their seriously understood relativity.

Brunner's personalistic approach primarily attributes evil to individuals, suggesting their behavior should be the starting point for change. This viewpoint, however, limits his insight into the structural form of evil, leading to a lack of critical engagement with social institutions.

In the face of Barth's critique, Brunner continued his approach of nature and grace. He emphasized "credo," subjective faith-appropriation, and sought lifelong dialogue with those outside the church. His eristic theology aims to elicit confession of untruth from humans, teaching them to understand their own questions about God correctly.

In his anthropology, Brunner adheres to Buber's philosophy of I-Thou, highlighting "responsibility" as the core of anthropology. He argues that the essence of humans lies in their relationship to the Thou, and this relationship is manifested through faith.

Brunner emphasizes the dynamism of faith, opposing the static nature of objective dogma. His concept of "Truth as Encounter" reflects the biblical concept of truth, depicting it as a historical and changing event, ultimately revealing God's self-disclosure.

His personal understanding of faith impacts his concept of the church. Brunner distinguishes between the institution of the church and the Ekklesia of the New Testament, describing the true church as a personal community of Christ.

Brunner criticizes the transformation of the Ekklesia into an institution over the course of church history. He believes that the institutional churches can't be transformed back into the Ekklesia but should at least not hinder its manifestation. He sees the ecumenical task not in the unity of the churches but in their "brotherly communion."

In sum, Emil Brunner's unique approach to religious philosophy and natural theology has left a significant imprint on the field of theology. His distinct understanding of the state, the orders of creation, and their relationship with sin offers a unique perspective on the interaction of the divine and the worldly. The dialectic he posits between acceptance and refusal, between the conservative and the revolutionary, offers a nuanced view of the human relationship with God's orders.

Brunner's personalistic approach, while insightful, has its limitations, particularly in addressing structural forms of evil. However, his emphasis on dialogue and engagement with those outside of the church reflects a commitment to a more inclusive and accessible theology.

His anthropological perspective, particularly his focus on responsibility and relationship as the essence of humanity, offers a thoughtful exploration of the human condition. His belief in the dynamism of faith and the concept of "Truth as Encounter" underscores his rejection of a static, objective faith.

Brunner's understanding of the church as a personal community of Christ rather than an institution highlights his emphasis on personal faith. While acknowledging the limitations of the institutional church, he urges it to facilitate the emergence of the true Ekklesia.

In closing, the impact of Emil Brunner's work extends beyond his lifetime, continuing to inspire and provoke thought among scholars today. His unique approach to religious-philosophical methods and natural theology not only enriched the dialectical theology movement but also continues to shape our understanding of faith, philosophy, and the human experience. His work is a testament to the profound and enduring influence of thoughtful, critical engagement with theological concepts.

ABOUT THE AUTHOR

THE WRITTEN ENDEAVORS OF Dr. Dong In Baek are akin to a symphony of intellect and spirituality, a testament to a life steeped in the pursuit of knowledge and devotion to faith. His academic sojourn, which includes a PhD in philosophy from the esteemed Johann Wolfgang Goethe University in Frankfurt, and an enriching exploration of political science at L'École des Hautes Études Politiques in Paris and St. Petersburg State University serves as the deep well from which he draws to nourish his writing.

In Dr. Baek's work, one can discern the echoes of his time in the lecture halls of Keimyung University in Korea, the seminar rooms of St. Petersburg State University in Russia, and the research labs of Yonsei University in Seoul, Korea. Every role he has embraced, whether as a visiting researcher at Seoul National University or as an adjunct professor at Faith International University in Tacoma, Washington, has left an indelible mark on his literary output.

Assuming the mantle of the chancellor of the Institute of Eastern and Western Societies at St. Petersburg State University has lent Dr. Baek a unique perspective. His writing reflects the breadth of his understanding, traversing the liminal spaces where cultural, political, and social systems meet, clash, and sometimes harmonize.

Yet, it is not solely the intellectual sphere that informs Dr. Baek's authorial voice. Woven through his academic discourse is the rich tapestry of his spiritual journey. As an ordained minister of the Seoul North Presbytery of the Presbyterian Church (Tonghap)

ABOUT THE AUTHOR

in Korea and a member of the Cascade of the Presbyterian Church (U.S.A.), his faith imbues his work with spiritual resonance. His writings are thus a confluence of philosophy, political science, and theology, a unique blend of academic rigor and spiritual depth, offering readers an enlightened path to traverse.

BIBLIOGRAPHY

Brunner, Emil. "Die andere Aufgabe der Theologie" ["The Other Task of Theology"]. *Zwischen den Zeiten* 7 (1929) 255–76.
———. "Begegnung mit Kierkegaard." *Journal of Theology and Church* 2 (1929) 45–63.
———. *Blätter für Deutsche Philosophie* 3 (1929/1930) 265–82.
———. "Die Botschaft Sören Kierkegaards' ["The Message of Søren Kierkegaard"]. *Neue Schweizer Rundschau* 23.2 (1930) 84–99.
———. *Die christliche Lehre von der Kirche, vom Glauben und von der Vollendung*. 2nd ed. Vol. 3 of *Dogmatik*. Zurich: 1964.
———. *Die christliche Lehre von Gott* [*The Christian Doctrine of God*]. 4th ed. Vol. 1 of *Dogmatik*. Zurich: 1972.
———. *Die christliche Lehre von Schöpfung und Erlösung* [*The Christian Doctrine of Creation and Redemption*]. 3rd ed. Vol. 2 of *Dogmatik*. Zurich: 1972.
———. "Die Christusbotschaft im Kampf mit den Religionen" ["The Message of Christ in the Struggle with Religions"]. *Basler Missions-studien* 8 (1931) 1–20.
———. "Das Elend der Theologie." *Kirchenblatt* (1920) 50–52.
———. *Erlebnis, Erkenntnis und Glaube* [*Experience, Knowledge, and Faith*]. Tübingen: 1921.
———. "Die Frage nach dem 'Anknüpfungspunkt' als Problem der Theologie" ["The Question of the 'Starting Point' as a Problem of Theology"]. *Zwischen den Zeiten* 10 (1932) 505–32.
———. *Das Gebot und die Ordnungen: Entwurf einer protestantisch-theologischen Ethik* [*The Commandment and the Orders: Outline of a Protestant Theological Ethic*]. Tübingen: 1932.
———. "Gesetz und Offenbarung: Eine theologische Grundlegung" ["Law and Revelation: A Theological Foundation"]. In *Anfänge der dialektischen Theologie*, by Karl Barth et al., edited by Jürgen Moltmann, 1:290–98. München: Chr. Kaiser, 1962.
———. *Gott und Mensch: Vier Untersuchungen über das personhafte Sein* [*God and Man: Four Investigations into Personal Being*]. Tübingen: 1930.

BIBLIOGRAPHY

———. *Die Grenzen der Humanität: Habilitationsvorlesung an der Universität Zürich* [*The Limits of Humanity: Postdoctoral Lectures at the University of Zurich*]. Sammlung gemeinverständlicher Vorträge und Schriften aus dem Gebiet der Theologie und Religionsgeschichte 102. Tübingen: 1922.

———. "Das Grundproblem der Philosophie bei Kant und Kierkegaard" ["The Basic Problem of Philosophy in Kant and Kierkegaard"]. *Zwischen den Zeiten* 2.6 (1924) 31–47.

———. "Die Kirche und die sozialen Forderungen der Gegenwart" ["The Church and the Social Demands of the Present"]. *Glarner Nachrichten*, Dec 16, 1918.

———. *Man in Revolt: A Christian Anthropology*. Translated by Olive Wyon. Philadelphia: Westminster, 1939.

———. *The Mediator: A Study of the Central Doctrine of the Christian Faith*. Philadelphia: Westminster, 1947.

———. *Der Mensch im Widerspruch* [*Man in Contradiction*]: *Die christliche Lehre vom wahren und vom wirklichen Menschen*. 4th ed. Zurich: 1965.

———. *Der Mittler: Zur Besinnung über den Christusglauben* [*The Mediator: A Study of the Central Doctrine of the Christian Faith*]. 2nd ed. Tübingen: 1930.

———. *Die Mystik und das Wort: Der Gegensatz zwischen moderner Religionsauffassung und christlichem Glauben dargestellt an der Theologie Schleiermachers*. [*Mysticism and the Word: The Antithesis between Modern Religious Conceptions and Christian Faith Presented in the Theology of Schleiermacher*]. 2nd ed. Tübingen: 1924.

———. *Natur und Gnade: Zum Gespräch mit Karl Barth* [*Nature and Grace: In Conversation with Karl Barth*]. 2nd ed. Tübingen: 1935.

———. "Der neue Barth: Bemerkungen zu Karl Barths Lehre vom Menschen" ["The New Barth: Remarks on Karl Barth's Doctrine of Man"]. *Zeitschrift für Theologie und Kirche* 48 (1951) 89–100.

———. "Die Offenbarung als Grund und Gegenstand der Theologie: Antrittsrede an der Universität Zürich" ["Revelation as the Foundation and Object of Theology. Inaugural address at the University of Zurich"]. *Philosophie und Offenbarung* (1925) 5–28.

———. *Offenbarung und Vernunft: Die Lehre von der christlichen Glaubenserkenntnis* [*Revelation and Reason: The Doctrine of Christian Knowledge*]. 2nd ed. Zurich: 1941.

———. *Religionsphilosophie protestantischer Theologie* [*Protestant Theology's Philosophy of Religion*]. Special edition of Handbuchs der Philosophie 2. Munich: 1927.

———. *Reformation und Romantik*. Vortrag, gehalten bei der Tagung der Luther-Gesellschaft in München am 18. München: Chr. Kaiser, 1925.

———. "*Der Römerbrief* von Karl Barth: Eine zeitgemäße unmoderne Paraphrase." *Kirchenblatt für die reformierte Schweiz* 34 (Feb 1919) 29–32.

———. "A Spiritual Autobiography." *Japan Christian Quarterly* (July 1955). 238–44.

BIBLIOGRAPHY

———. *Das Symbolische in der religiösen Erkenntnis: Beiträge zu einer Theorie der religiösen Erkenntnis*. Tübingen: 1914.
———. *The Theology of Crisis*. New York: Charles Scribner, 1929.
———. "Theologie und Kirche" ["Theology and Church"]. *Zwischen den Zeiten* 8 (1930) 397–420.
———. *Wahrheit als Begegnung: Sechs Vorlesungen über das christliche Wahrheitsverständnis* [*Truth as Encounter: Six Lectures on the Christian Understanding of Truth*]. Berlin: 1938.

FURTHER LITERATURE

Aquinas, Thomas. *Summa theologia*. Edited by Katholischen Akademikverband. Die deutsche Thomas-Ausgabe. 3rd ed. Salzburg: Anton Pustet, 1934ff.
Aristoteles. *Eth. Nik.* In *Hauptwerke*, edited by W. Nestle. KTA 129. Stuttgart: Kober, 1968.
———. *Politik*. In *Hauptwerke*, edited by W. Nestle. KTA 129. Stuttgart: Kober, 1968.
Barth, Heinrich. "Gotteserkenntnis" ["The Knowledge of God"]. In *Anfänge der dialektischen Theologie*, edited by Jürgen Moltmann, 1:221–56. Munich: Chr. Kaiser, 1977.
Barth, Karl. "Abschied" ["Farewell"]. *Zwischen den Zeiten* 11 (1933) 536–44. And in *Theologische Existenz heute* 7 (1934).
———. "Der Christ in der Gesellschaft" ["Christian in Society"]. In *Anfänge der dialektischen Theologie* 1:5–6. Edited by Jürgen Moltmann. 5th ed. Munich: Chr. Kaiser, 1985.
———. "Brunners Schleiermacherbuch." *Zwischen den Zeiten* 8 (1924) 49–64.
———. *Die Kirchliche Dogmatik*. 13 vols. Zurich: 1932–59.
———. *Die Menschlichkeit Gottes* [*The Humanity of God*]. Zurich: 1956.
———. "Nein! Antwort an Emil Brunner" ["No! Response to Emil Brunner"]. In *Scheidung und Bewährung*, edited by W. Fürst, 208–58. Theologische Buchreihe 34. 1966.
———. *Der Römerbrief*. Reprint, Zurich: 1963.
———. "Die Theologie und die Mission in der Gegenwart ["Theology and Mission in the Present"]: Vortrag gehalten an der Brandenburgischen Missionskonferenz in Berlin am 11. April 1932." In *Theologische Fragen und Antworten. Gesammelte Vorträge*, 3:100–26. Zollikon: Evangelischer, 1957.
———. "Das Wort Gottes als Aufgabe der Theologie: Vortrag für die Versammlung der 'Freunde der Christlichen Welt' auf der Elgersburg im Oktober 1922" ["The Word of God as a Task of Theology. Lecture for the Meeting of the 'Friends of the Christian World' at Elgersburg in October 1922"]. *Christliche Welt* 36 (1922).

BIBLIOGRAPHY

———, and Eduard Thurneysen. *Karl Barth–Eduard Thurneysen Briefwechsel [Correspondence]*. Band 2: *1921–1930*. Edited by Eduard Thurneysen. In *Karl Barth Gesamtausgabe V. Briefe*. Zurich: Theologischer, 1974.

Barth, Karl, et al. *Anfänge der dialektischen Theologie I*. Edited by Jürgen Moltmann. 5th ed. Munich: Chr. Kaiser, 1985.

Bergson, Henri. *Einführung in die Metaphysik [Introduction to Metaphysics]*. Jena: E. Diederich, 1909.

Betz, Hans Dieter, et al., eds. *Die Religion in Geschichte und Gegenwart: Handwörterbuch für Theologie und Religionswissenschaft [Religion Past and Present: Handbook for Theology and Religious Studies]*. 6 vols. 3rd ed. Tübingen: Mohr Siebeck, 1957-62.

Bonhoeffer, Dietrich. *Ethik*. Edited by Eberhard Bethge. 6th ed. Munich: Chr. Kaiser, 1963.

———. *Nachfolge*. 11th ed. Munich: Chr. Kaiser 1976.

Buber, Martin. *Ich und Du*. Leipzig: 1923.

Calvin, Johannes. *Institutio Christianae Religionis* 1559. Edited by Peter Barth and Wilhelm Niesel. Ioannis Calvini Opera Selecta 3-5. Munich: Chr. Kaiser, 1952-62.

———. *Ioannis Calvini: Opera quae supersunt omnia*. Edited by Wilhelm Baum et al. 59 vols. Corpus Reformatorum 29-87. Brunswick and Berlin: Schwetschke, 1863-1900.

Cullberg, John. "Das Du und die Wirklichkeit." *Zeitschrift für Theologie und Kirche, Neue Folge* (1933) 14-41. Edited by H. E. Eisenhuth.

Denzinger, Heinrich, and Adolf Schönmetzer. *Enchiridion symbolorum: Definitionum et declarationum de rebus fidei et morum [Enchiridion Symbolorum: A Compendium of Creeds, Definitions, and Declarations on Matters of Faith and Morals]*. 34th ed. Freiburg: 1967.

Ebeling, Gerhard. "Die Evidenz des Ethischen und die Theologie." *Zeitschrift für Theologie und Kirche* 57.3 (Jan 1960) 318-56.

Ebner, Ferdinand. *Das Wort und die geistigen Realitäten: Pneumatologische Fragmente [The Word and Spiritual Realities: Pneumatological Fragments]*. (1921). In *Schriften* vol. 1: *Fragmente. Aufsätze. Aphorismen. Zu einer Pneumatologie des Wortes [Fragments. Essays. Aphorisms. Towards a Pneumatology of the Word]*. Munich: Seyr, 1963-65.

———. *Schriften* vol. 2: *Notizen. Tagebücher. Lebenserinnerungen*. Munich: Kösel, 1963.

Fichte, Johann Gottlieb. *Die Anweisung zum seligen Leben, oder auch die Religionslehre 6. Vorlesung, 1806 [The Way to the Blessed Life, or the Doctrine of Religion, Sixth Lecture, 1806]*. In *J. G. Fichtes Sämtliche Werke* 5, edited by I. H. Fichte, 485. Berlin: Fichte, 1845.

Franken, Johannes Christiaan. *Kritische Philosophie und dialektische Theologie. Prolegomena zu einer philosophischen Behandlung des Problems der christlichen Gemeinschaft*. Amsterdam: H. J. Paris, 1932.

BIBLIOGRAPHY

Ganoczy, Alexandre. *Ecclesia ministrans: Dienende Kirche und kirchlicher Dienst bei Calvin* [*Ecclesia Ministrans: Serving Church and Ecclesiastical Service in Calvin*]. Translated by Hans Sayer. Freiburg: 1968.

Gestrich, Christof. *Neuzeitliches Denken und die Spaltung der dialektischen Theologie: Zur Frage der natürlichen Theologie* [*Modern Thought and the Division of Dialectical Theology: On the Question of Natural Theology*]. Beiträge zur historischen Theologie 52. Tübingen: 1977.

Gyllenberg, Rafael. *Reunamuistutuksia barthilaiseen teologiaan* [*Marginal Notes on Barthian Theology*]. Vartija: 1926.

Hegel, Georg Wilhelm Friedrich. *Enzyklopädie der philosophischen Wissenschaften im Grundriss.* 4th ed. Berlin: 1845.

Heim, Karl. *Glaube und Denken: Philosophische Grundlegung einer christlichen Lebensanschauung.* Berlin: Furche, 1931.

Hirschberger, Johannes. *Geschichte der Philosophie.* 2 vols. 8th ed. Freiburg: 1965.

Höfer, Josef, and Karl Rahner, eds. *Lexikon für Theologie und Kirche.* 10 vols. 2nd ed. Freiburg: 1957-65.

Hummel, G. *Theologische Anthropologie und die Wirklichkeit der Psyche: Zum Gespräch zwischen Theologie und analytischer Psychologie* [*Theological Anthropology and the Reality of the Psyche. On the Conversation between Theology and Analytical Psychology*]. Darmstadt: 1972.

Jalkanen, Kaarlo Väinö Lemmitty. *1909-1924.* Vol. 1 of *Karl Barth in käsitys teologian tehtavasta* [*Karl Barth's Assessment of the Task of Theology*]. Helsinki: Suomalainen Teologinen Kirjallisuusseura, 1947.

Kähler, Martin. *Die Wissenschaft der christlichen Lehre, von dem evangelischen Grundartikel aus im Abriss dargestellt* [*The Science of Christian Doctrine, Outlined from the Evangelical Fundamental Article*]. 3rd ed. Erlangen: Andreas Deichert, 1903.

Kant, Immanuel. *Grundlegung zur Metaphysik der Sitten* [*Groundwork of the Metaphysics of Morals*]. Edited by K. Vorländer. Hamburg: 1952.

―――. *Kritik der reinen Vernunft* [*Critique of Pure Reason*]. Edited by E. Adickes. Berlin: 1889.

―――. *Die Religion innerhalb der Grenzen der bloßen Vernunft* [*Religion within the Limits of Reason Alone*]. Edited by K. Kehrbach. Leipzig: n.d.

Karrer, Otto. *Um die Einheit der Christen: Die Petrusfrage; Ein Gespräch mit Emil Brunner, Oscar Cullman, and Hans v. Campenhausen.* Frankfurt: Knecht, 1953.

Kern, Walter. "Das Verhältnis von Erkenntnis und Liebe als philosophisches Grundproblem bei Hegel und Thomas von Aquin" ["The Relationship between Knowledge and Love as a Fundamental Philosophical Problem in Hegel and Thomas Aquinas"]. *Scholasticism* 34 (1959) 394-427.

König, Albert. "Emil Brunners Staatsauffassung und der Universalismus Othmar Spanns." PhD diss., Universität Leipzig, 1938.

Krause, Gerhard, and Gerhard Müller, eds. *Theologische Realenzyklopädie.* Vol 7, *Böhmische Brüder—Chinesische Religion.* Berlin: De Gruyter, 1981.

BIBLIOGRAPHY

Kreck, W. *Basic Decisions in Karl Barth's Dogmatics*. Neukirchen: 1978.

Küng, Hans. *On Being a Christian*. New York: 1976.

Lakebrink, Bernhard. *Hegels dialektische Ontologie und die thomistische Analektik*. Cologne: 1955.

Leipold, Heinrich. *Missionarische Theologie: Emil-Brunners-Weg zur theologische Anthropologie* [*Missionary Theology: Emil Brunner's Path to Theological Anthropology*]. Göttingen: 1974.

Luther, Martin. *De servo arbitrio*. In Weimarer Ausgabe, 18:754.36–38. Weimar: Hermann Böhlaus Nachfolger, 1826–57.

Marquardt, Friedrich-Wilhelm. "Der Aktuar: Aus Barths Pfarramt." In *Einwürfe* 3, edited by Friedrich-Wilhelm Marquardtet al., 93–139. München: Chr. Kaiser, 1986.

———. *Der Christ in der Gesellschaft: 1919–1979; Geschichte, Analysen und aktuelle Bedeutung von Karl Barths Tombach Vortrag*. Theologische Existenz heute 206 (1986).

———. *Religionskritik und Entmythologisierung: Über einen Beitrag Karl Barths zur Entmythologisierungsfrage*. Munich: 1968.

Meyer, Hermann Julius. "Heros." In *Meyer's Konversations-Lexikon. Eine Encyklopädie des Allgemeinen Wissens*; Irideen-Königsgrün, 5th ed. Leipzig: Bibliographisches Institut, 1896–1900.

Moltmann, Jürgen. "Der Mensch." In *Systematic Theology*, 157–58. Munich: Christian Kaiser, 1983.

Nygren, Anders. *Dogmatikens vetenskapliga grundläggning* [*Scientific Foundations of Dogmatics*]. Lund: 1922.

———. *Eros und Agape: Gestaltwandlungen der christlichen Liebe*. Translated by P. S. Watson. 2nd ed. Gütersloh: 1954.

Otte, Klaus. "Gnade V." In *Theologische Realenzyklopädie*, 8:496–511.

———. *Lernen als reflexiv vollzogene Existenz: Die Analyse eines Lernprozesses in der Theologie dargestellt anhand von Karl Rahners Das Leben der Toten* [*Learning as Reflexive Existence, The Analysis of a Learning Process in Theology Presented on Karl Rahner's The Life of the Dead*]. Neuausgabe: Peter Lang, 1978.

Overbeck, Franz. *Christentum und Kultur: Gedanken und Anmerkungen zur modernen Theologie* [*Christianity and Culture: Thoughts and Notes on Modern Theology*]. Darmstadt: Wissenschaftlich, 1963.

Pannenberg, Wolfhart. *Basic Questions in Theology: Collected Essays*. Vol. 1. Louisville: Westminster John Knox, 1990.

———. *Grundzüge der Christologie* [*Basic Questions in Theology*]. Gütersloh: 1964.

Ritschl, Albrecht. *Die positive Entwicklung der Lehre* [*The Positive Development of Teaching*]. Vol. 3 of *Die christliche Lehre von der Rechtfertigung und Versöhnung* [*Christian Doctrine of Justification and Reconciliation*]. 4th ed. Bonn: 1895.

BIBLIOGRAPHY

Roessler, Roman. *Person und Glaube: Der Personalismus der Gottesbeziehung bei Emil Brunner.* Munich: 1965.

Salakka, Yrjö. *Person und Offenbarung in der Theologie Emil Brunners während der Jahre 1914-1937* [*Person and Revelation in Emil Brunner's Theology during the Years 1914-1937*]. Schriften der Luther-Agricola-Gesellschaft 12. Helsinki: 1960.

Scheld, Stefan. *Die Christologie Emil Brunners: Beitrag zur Überwindung liberaler Jesulogie und dialektisch-doketischer Christologie im Zuge geschichtlich-dialogischen Denkens.* Wiesbaden: 1981.

Schier, Wolfgang. "Der Staat in der Theologie Emil Brunners unter bes. Berücksichtigung des Schöpfungsgedankens im Vergleich mit der evangelischen Theologie der Gegenwart." PhD diss., Ludwig-Maximilians-Universität, München, 1950.

Schleiermacher, Friedrich. *Der christliche Glaube, nach den Grundsätzen der evangelischen Kirche im Zusammenhang dargestellt.* Edited by Martin Redeker. 2 vols. 7th ed. Berlin: De Gruyter, 1960.

―――. *Über die Religion: Reden an die Gebildeten unter ihren Verächtern.* Edited by Karl Schwarz. Leipzig: F. A. Brockhaus, 1868.

―――. "Über seine Glaubenslehre an Herrn Dr. Lücke." In *Schleiermacher: Auswahl,* edited by H. Bolli, 120-75. Munich: 1968.

Schmitt, R., ed. *Die deutsche Philosophie der Gegenwart in Selbstdarstellungen* [*Contemporary German Philosophy in Self-Portrayals*]. Vol. 1. 1921.

Schröder, Gerhardt. "Das Ich und das Du in der Wende des Denkens: Untersuchung zum Aufbruch der Ich-Du-Problematik und ihrer Verwendung bei Gogarten und Brunner." PhD diss., Kiel, 1948.

Soden, Hans von. *Theologie und Kirche in Werken Hans von Sodens: Briefe und Dokumente aus der Zeit des Kirchenkampfes, 1933-1945.* Edited by Erich Dinkler and Erika Dinkler-von Schubert, with Michael Wolter. Arbeiten zur kirchlichen Zeitgeschichte, Reihe A, Quellen; Bd. 2. Göttingen: Vandenhoeck und Ruprecht, 1986.

Spiegel, Yorick. *Theologie der bürgerlichen Gesellschaft: Sozialphilosophie und Glaubenslehre bei Friedrich Schleiermacher* [*Theology of Civil Society*]. Munich: 1968.

Stange, Carl. *Christentum und moderne Weltanschauung* [*Christianity and Modern Worldview*]. Leipzig: 1911.

―――. "Natürliche Theologie: Zur Krisis der dialektischen Theologie." *Zeitschrift für Systematische Theologie (ZSTh)* 12 (1935) 367-452.

Staudenmaier, Franz Anton. *Darstellung und Kritik des Hegelschen Systems aus den Standpunkten der christlichen Philosophie.* Mainz: 1844.

Stolz, Wilhelm. *Theologie, dialektischer Personalismus und kirchliche Einheit: Apologetisch-kritische Studie zu Emil Brunners Lehre von der Kirche im Lichte der thomistischen Theologie.* Freiburg, Switzerland: Universitätsverlag, 1953.

Thielicke, Helmut. *Prolegomena: Die Beziehung der Theologie zu den Denkformen der Neuzeit* [*Introduction: The Relationship of Theology to*

Modern Thought]. Vol. 1 of *Der evangelische Glaube: Grundzüge der Dogmatik* [*The Evangelical Faith: An Outline of Christian Dogmatics*]. Tübingen: 1968.

———. *Introduction: The Relationship of Theology to Modern Thought*. Vol. 1 of *The Evangelical Faith: An Outline of Christian Dogmatics*. Grand Rapids: Eerdmans, 1974-1976.

Troeltsch, Ernst. "Offenbarung." In *Die Religion in Geschichte und Gegenwart: Handwörterbuch für Theologie und Religionswissenschaft* 4. 6 vols. Tübingen: 1909-13.

———. *Psychologie und Erkenntnistheorie in der Religionswissenschaft* [*Psychology and Epistemology in the Study of Religion*]. Tübingen: 1905.

Ulrich, Hans, ed. *Theologie und Ökonomie: Symposium zum 100. Geburtstag von Emil Brunner*. Zurich: Ruh, 1992.

Vogelsanger, Peter, ed. *Der Auftrag der Kirche in der modernen Welt: Festgabe für Emil Brunner*. Zurich: Vogelsanger, 1959.

Volkelt, J. *Die Gefühlsgewissheit* [*The Certainty of Feeling*]. Munich: 1922.

Volken, Lorenz. *Der Glaube bei Emil Brunner*. Freiburg: 1947.

Volk, Hermann. "Die Christologie bei Karl Barth und Emil Brunner." In *Das Konzil von Chalkedon*, 3:613-73.

———. "Emil Brunners Lehre von der ursprünglichen Gottebenbildlichkeit des Menschen." PhD diss., Münster, 1939.

Christliche Studentenkonferenz. Vorträge auf der Aarauer Studentenkonferenz [Lectures at the Aarau Student Conference] 5-34. Basel: 1919.

Weber, Otto. *Grundlagen der Dogmatik* [*Foundations of Dogmatics*]. Vol. 1. 5th ed. Neukirchen: 1977.

Wegscheider, Julius August Ludwig. *Institutiones theologiae christianae dogmaticae*. 1815.

Windelband, W. *The Sacred in Preludes*. Tübingen: 1915.

INDEX

Aarau Student Conference, 31–32
Absolute, xvi, 14, 15, 85
absolute dependence, 10, 38n30
absoluteness, 9–10, 17–18, 29, 56, 60
active intellect *(nous poietikos)*, 8
activity of God, 25
Adam, xviii, 95
affinity, 21–22, 29
agnosticism, 84, 84n42
Ahasverus, 34
Althaus, Paul, 105
ambivalent or transcending character of the symbol, 25
analogia entis, 58n117
analogy, 22–23, 30, 36–44, 45, 70n168, 77
anthropology, 47–48, 52, 61, 65, 68, 72, 76, 77, 77n205, 80–81, 84, 86–90, 105, 107–8
anti-intellectualism, Bergson, 34
apologetics, 73–74
Aquinas, Thomas, 22–23
archetype, Schleiermacher's concept of, 81–82
Aristotelian–Scholastic philosophy, 8, 28
Aristotle, 8–9, 23, 67
Augustine, 23, 62
autonomy, 6, 6n12, 11, 81, 85, 88, 104
awareness of God, 1, 24, 90
awareness of moral norms, 12, 18

Balthasar, 100
Barth, Heinrich, 31–32
Barth, Karl, 4, 32–33, 45–46, 55–56n104
  critical engagement with Brunner, xvi–xvii, 58n117, 61, 76–77, 77n205, 96–101
  dialectical relationship between God and man, 90
  dialectical theology, xv, 35, 43, 45–46, 104
  The Epistle to the Romans, 32n5, 33, 35, 38n33, 46, 46n64
  eristics/eristic theology, 63n138, 69n163, 75–76
  grace, 1–2
  imago Dei, 53n93, 92–94
  natural theology, 78
  "No!," 70n173, 105
  "other task of theology," 75n194
  point of connection, 90–91
  psychologism, 36–38, 46n64
  and Schleiermacher, 38n30
  theological objectivism, 62n131
  Tombach lecture, 32n5
  transformation to the I-Thou relationship, 65–71
believing thinking, 65
Berger-Gebhardt, Ursula, 100
Bergson, Henri, xvi, 6–7, 6n12, 12, 24n107, 27, 33–34, 67
Between the Times (journal), 77
Bible, 73, 94
biblical truth, 86, 94, 107

INDEX

biblical understanding of revelation, 2, 54
bios theoretikos, 84
Blumhardt, Christoph, 45, 63n138
Bonhoeffer, Dietrich, 1, 1n3
Buber, Martin, xvii, 40n43, 43n53, 43n54, 61, 62, 66, 97, 107
Bultmann, Rudolf, 47, 62, 89, 104

Calvin, John, xvi, 15, 53, 68
categorical imperatives, 11, 17, 85, 92
causality, 9, 17, 32, 81
character of revelation, 64, 71
Christian faith, 39-40, 49-54, 56-60, 68, 75, 85
Christian knowledge of man, 86-88
Christian truth, 62n131, 95, 101
Christocentric approaches, 77n205, 95
Christology, xv, 32n5, 48n68, 52, 55, 59-60, 100-101. See also *The Mediator* (Brunner)
Church Times, 100
cognition, tool of, 28
The Commandment and the Orders (Brunner), 103
community, 82, 97, 105-6
confrontational address of God's word, 94
connection, point of, 3, 20n85, 46, 48, 56n104, 73-74, 90-91, 99, 104-5
consciousness, religious. See religious consciousness
consciousness of absolute being, 9-10
consciousness of responsibility, 90-92
consciousness theology, xvi, 13, 23-24
contemporaneity, Kierkegaard, xviii
continuity, 35, 39, 55, 85-86

contradiction of creation and sin, 86-90, 87n56, 93
corruption, 87-88, 93
creation, xviii, 50, 52, 56n104, 63, 86-90, 95, 97
creation orders, 70n173, 101, 105-8

decision-making, 64, 68, 73-77, 96, 101
dependence, 10-11, 17, 28, 30, 57, 59
determinism, 74-75
dialectical relationship between connection and opposition, 91
dialectical theology, xv-xvii, 9, 35, 39, 43, 45-46, 47, 55, 55-56n104, 61, 77, 86, 88-90, 103-8
dialectic between God and humanity, 41-42, 86-90
"Dialectic of Love" (Küng), 9n25
dialogical thinking/theology, xvii, 43, 66-68, 74, 76-77, 94, 96
diversity, 17, 29
divine, transcendence of, 19-20
divine-human dialogue, 2, 66
divine message, 63, 80, 82
divine truth, 40-42, 49-50, 66
divinity of Jesus, 44, 45, 53-54, 57, 59, 83
doctrine of opposition, 86-88
doctrine of origin, 86-88
doctrine of the reality of man, 86-88
dogmatics, xviii, 1, 64, 88
Dogmatics (Brunner), 61, 61n130
dwelling of God, 19, 27

Ebner, Ferdinand, xvii, 40n43, 43n53, 43n54, 61, 62, 66-67, 97
ego and God, 20

INDEX

Ekklesia of the New Testament, 107–8
Elert, Werner, 105
emotional intuition, 32
empirical appearance, 18–19
"Epilogue for Theologians" (Brunner), 37
epistemological approaches, 11, 28–30
epistemological intellectualism, 7, 27
The Epistle to the Romans (Barth), 32n5, 33, 35, 38n33, 46, 46n64
equality, 22–23, 29
eristics/eristic theology, 1, 61–65, 61n130, 63n138, 65n143, 69n163, 75–76, 75n194, 79, 96, 107
essence of religion, 18–19, 57
ethical objectivism, Kant, 32
ethics, xvii, 6, 11, 18, 30, 83, 101
evil, 38–39, 85, 107–8
existence, 72, 72n178
existential dialectic, Kierkegaard, 43n53
existential revelation, xviii
Experience, Knowledge, and Faith (Brunner), 33, 33n7, 44–45, 56–58, 65–66, 103
expression function of symbols, 21–24, 29
external contradictions, 88

faith, xvi, 5, 15, 32n5, 36–44, 41n44, 47–48, 59–60, 64–69, 71–73, 76, 79–82, 85–86, 94–95, 105–8
false humanism, 88
Father, correlation concept to heaven, 27
Feuerbach, Ludwig, 41–42, 67
Fichte, Johann Gottlieb, 31–32, 50
First Vatican Council, 49n73
First World War, 45

folk religions, 49–51
formal imago Dei, xviii, 91–92, 96–98
freedom, 11, 17

general Logos *(Logos asarkos)*, 99–100
general religion, 39, 49–50, 56, 81
general revelation, xviii, 48, 49–51, 54, 78, 97
Gestrich, Christof, 67
God
  absolute claim, xvii, 5
  dialectical relationship with man, 86–90
  dialectical theology, 104–8
  ego, 20
  image of God/imago Dei, xvii–xviii, 2, 43n52, 45, 53n93, 86–89, 90–94, 96–99
  immanence of in consciousness, 19
  intellectualism, 9
  knowledge of, 19
  natural theology, 78
  objectifying thinking about, 36n22, 72
  religious and theological psychologism, 36–44
  "other task of theology," 72–77
  religious knowledge, 21–30
  self-revelation, 54–58, 94, 104
  special revelation, 47–60
  theology of revelation, 96–101
  transcendence, 17, 19–20
  transformation to the I-Thou relationship, 65–71
  true personal encounter, 94–95
  unbroken connection with humanity, 83–86
God and man, 19, 27, 45, 55, 61, 62n131, 65–70, 72, 90
God and Man (Brunner), 95
God-human, 25, 29, 38, 41n44, 92
God's revelation, 52, 63n138, 104

121

INDEX

Gogarten, Friedrich, 33, 40n43, 43n54, 46, 47, 56n104, 62, 97
grace, 1-2, 1n3, 2n7, 3, 48, 101, 107
Griesebach, Eberhard, 43n54

habilitation thesis, Brunner, 37
Hamann, Johann Georg, 62
Harnack, Adolf von, 5, 48, 59-60
hearing the gospel, 98-99
heaven, symbol of, 26-27, 29
Hegel, Georg Wilhelm Friedrich, 8-9, 9n25, 28, 67, 85-86, 85n51
Heidegger, Martin, 62
historical Jesus, 44, 79, 95, 99
historical and biblical truth, 86
historicism, 32, 39, 85
history/historical facts, 39-44, 50, 95
history, Hegel's philosophy of, 85-86, 85n51
Holy Spirit, 65-68
human behavior, 38, 93, 107
human condition, xvii, 106, 108
human existence, 39, 47, 55, 80, 85, 87, 89, 105
human experience, 12, 36, 53-54
humanity, 24-27, 47, 50, 52-53, 62-64, 71, 74, 75-77, 80-81, 93, 95, 96-100, 104, 108
humanity of Jesus, 53, 60, 73
human knowledge, 49, 80-81, 95
human nature, xvii, 87n56, 93
human reason, 71, 75, 83-86
human situation and divine message, 63, 82
human unbelief, 56, 65, 73, 76, 79-80, 105
hypostatic union, 53

ideal image, 81-82
idealism, 6, 6n12, 27, 82, 85, 88, 104

identity with God, consciousness of, 19
illusionism, 5, 11, 28, 82
image of God/imago Dei, xvii-xviii, 2, 43n52, 45, 53n93, 86-89, 90-94, 96-99
immanence, 19-20, 20n85, 27, 29-30, 36, 41, 84n42
immanent evolution, 85
immanent religion, 54
immediacy, 34
incarnation of God, 2, 50, 93
individualism, 25-26
individualistic, privatizing understanding of religion, 14, 28
infinite moral spirit, 18
inner contradiction in man, 88
inner vision. *See* intuition
institutional churches, 107-8
intellectualism, 8-13, 31-35, 36, 38
intellectual-speculative, 38
intelligible self, freedom of the, 11
interiority, 33-34, 70n173
intuition, xvi, 7, 8-13, 13-16, 16-19, 21-23, 27-30, 32-33
intuitive knowledge, xvi, 15, 27-28
intuitive self-reflection, 13-14, 28-29
irrationalism, 84
I-Thou relationship, xvii, 42-43, 43n53, 61, 65-71, 107

Jalkanen, Kaarlo Väinö Lemmitty, 46n64
Jesus Christ, xviii, 2, 44, 45, 47, 50-54, 56-60, 70n168, 73, 78-83, 91-92, 95, 99-100, 107-8
John, 54
judgments, 8
justification doctrine of Luther, 38

INDEX

Kaftan, Julius, 5
Kähler, Martin, 90, 95
Kant, Immanuel, 5–6, 10–12, 14–15, 27–30, 31–32, 51, 85, 85n46
Kern, Walter, 9n25
Kierkegaard, Søren, xviii, 40, 43n53, 62, 66n148, 104
kingdom of God, 26–27, 29, 106
knowledge, xvi, 4–7, 8–13, 27–30, 47–48, 79–80, 98n7
knowledge of faith, 72n178
knowledge of God, 17–19, 30, 43, 48–54, 60, 70n168, 70n173, 98–99
"The Knowledge of God" (Barth), 31
Küng, Hans, 9n25
Künneth, Walter, 105
Kutter, Hermann, 5, 45

language of the ineffable, 24
law and commandment, 105
laws of creation, 97, 101
liberal theology, xv, xviii, 48
likeness to God, 87, 104, 105
limitations, 17, 108
"The Limits of Humanity" (Brunner), 37
logical laws, 9
Logos, 34–35, 50–51
love, 62–63, 91–92, 105
Luther, Martin, 38, 40n43, 74–75, 97
Lutheran doctrine, 1

man. *See* God and man
Man in Revolt (Brunner), xvii, 43n54, 60n128, 86, 87n56, 96–97
Marburg School, 31
material imago Dei, xviii, 53n93, 91–92, 96–97
mediation, xv, xvii, 16, 39, 86

The Mediator (Brunner), xvii, 48, 48n68, 49n71, 55, 60, 62, 67, 98n7, 103
Merz, G., 46
The Message of Christ in the Struggle with Religions (Brunner), 68
"The Misery of Theology" (Brunner), 32, 84
missionary theology, 65n143, 90–91
modern natural theology, xvii, 78–95
modern theology, 32, 48, 54–60, 80, 83
morality, 5–6, 10, 11, 12–13, 17–18, 24–25, 26, 28, 29–30, 51, 82–83, 84–85, 90, 97
mystery of man, 87–88
mystical-inner, 38
mystical-subjective experience, Schleiermacher, 32
mysticism, 14–15, 84, 84n42, 104
Mysticism and the Word (Brunner), xv, 103

natural revelation, 51–52, 104
natural theology, xv, 52, 58n117, 69–71, 70n169, 78–95, 100, 104, 106–8
nature, 1, 3, 5, 55, 78, 107
Natur und Gnade (Brunner), 53, 69, 77
Neo-Kantianism, 62
"No!" (Barth), 70n173, 105
norms, 17–18

obedience of faith, 76
obedience to God, 104
objective consciousness, 7, 21n89, 28
objective possibility for divine revelation, 2, 93–94
objective revelation, 15–16
objectivity, 19, 45

INDEX

objectivity of faith, 36, 40–42, 45
objectivity of God, 24, 27, 45
object of faith, 54, 66
Obstalden, 31, 103
opposition, 32n3, 48, 88–90, 105
original sin, 95, 104
"other task of theology," 2, 61, 71–77, 101
"The Other Task of Theology" (Brunner), 52, 64, 68
Otte, Klaus, 12n39
Otto, Rudolf, 60
Overbeck, Franz, 39

paradoxical-dialectical character, 89
participation, 23, 30
Pascal, Blaise, 45, 62
passive intellect *(nous pathetikos)*, 8
Paul, 79
personal being, 25, 42–43, 92
personal community of Christ, 107–8
personal encounter, 94–95
personality, 14, 20, 20n85, 24–26, 29, 73
personhood, xviii, 62, 92–93, 100, 101
Person-Truth, 94
Philosophy of Religion in Protestant Theology (Brunner), 103
piety/pious feeling, 11, 37, 39, 81
Plato, 23, 31–32, 35, 54
polemics/polemical theology, 64, 75
power, 97
practical reason, 5–6, 10, 85
preaching, 15, 75–76
pre-Christian revelation, 65
precondition, 50
presence of God as an object, 25
preservation grace of Christ, 98
primus inter pares, 78, 80
proclamation, 61, 75–76

profane symbols, 41
Protestant Church, 77
Protestant Theology's Philosophy of Religion (Brunner), 67
psychic phenomena, 23
psychologism, 32, 32n5, 36–44, 38n33, 46n64
pure objectivity, 41–42, 45

Ragaz, Leonhard, 4–5, 45
Rahner, Karl, 12, 12n39
ratio cognoscendi and *essendi*, 92
rationalism, 31
rationalistic theology, 51, 56
rational justification, Kant, 5, 18
rational truth, 89
reality of God, 20, 27
reason, 34, 58n117, 70, 74, 79–80, 89, 104
recognition, 8–9, 14, 19–20, 105–6
reconciliation, 50, 104
redemption, 56n104, 57, 98, 106
Reformation, 48, 69
relational equality, 23
relationality in revelation, 93
relationship with God, 14, 43n52, 52, 74, 108
religion, 9–11, 13–15, 37, 51, 54–60, 90
religious consciousness, 4–6, 8, 13–14, 17–20, 20n85, 24–26, 27–30
Religious Decision (Gogarten), 33
religious experience, 15–16, 18–20, 19n78
religious feeling, 37, 56
religious heroes, 14, 16, 30, 57
religious intellectualism, Hegel, 9
religious intuition, xvi, 12–13, 16, 28
religious knowledge, 4–5, 7, 8–13, 13–16, 17, 20, 21–27, 27–30, 42, 71–72, 83
religious personalities, 14, 28

INDEX

religious primordial act, 13–14, 28
religious socialism, xv, 45
religious subjectivism, 38
religious truth, 82–83
religious world, 12–13, 14, 28
"Response to Emil Brunner" (Barth), 70
responsible personal being, 92
revelation, theology of, xvi–xviii, 54n96, 61n130, 96–101, 104
   Christian faith, 68
   continuity in Brunner's thinking, 61–65
   double understanding of, 97–98, 98n7
   and faith, 65–66
   First Vatican Council on natural revelation, 49n73
   general revelation, xviii, 48, 49–51, 54, 78, 97
   imago Dei, 90–94
   knowledge of God through revelation in nature, 48–54
   mysticism, 15
   premise of thought, 78–83
   rational truth, 89
   and reason, 70–71
   special revelation, 47–60, 78
   unbroken connection between God and humanity, 83–86
Revelation and Reason (Brunner), 58n117, 98n7
righteousness given by Christ in faith, 85
Ritschl, Albrecht, 26, 40–41, 48, 57, 59, 80n10, 82–83
romantic mysticism, 57

Sacred in Preludes (Windelband), 19n78
Schlatter, Adolf, 4
Schleiermacher, Friedrich, xv–xvi, 1, 5, 7n16, 10–11, 27–28, 30, 32, 32n3, 37–38, 38n30, 40–41, 48, 55–56, 59–60, 69n163, 80n10, 80n13, 81–82, 84
Schmitt, R., 35n18
Scholasticism, 8
Scripture, 15
self-awareness, 9
self-consciousness, 12, 24n107
self-contradictions, 75
self-evaluation of humans, 13, 28
self-forgetful hearing of God, 38
self-knowledge, 54
self-reflection, 13–14, 28–29, 35, 64, 82
self-revelation of God, 54–58, 94, 104
self-understanding, 31, 55, 64, 71
Semi-Pelagians, 76
senses, 8
separation from God, 87
sermon, 75–76
sign function, 21, 29
similarity, 29–30
sin, xvii–xviii, 38–39, 53n93, 58, 69, 80–81, 86–90, 95, 97, 99, 106
social institutions, 106–8
sola gratia, 69, 71
soul, 23–24
special revelation, 47–60, 78
Spiegel, Yorick, 1, 32n3, 37–38n30
spiritual aspects of human beings, 29
spiritual certainty, 17, 29
spiritual life, 14, 19, 23, 24, 34, 36
spiritual-moral realm, 24
spiritual order, 29–30
spiritual personality, 17–18, 25
spiritual supraworld, xvi, 16–20, 24
spiritual transcendent, 24, 29
spiritual world, 25
subject and object of religious intuition, 12–13, 16, 28
subjective natural theology, 80–81
subjectivity, 27, 31, 67–68, 97

INDEX

subject-object opposition, 94
superhuman personality, 25, 29
supra-human personality, xvi, 16–20, 24
supra-individual spirit, 26
supra-world, 16–20
symbol consciousness, 21, 24
"The Symbolic in Religious Knowledge" (Brunner), xvi, 4, 4n1, 27
symbolism, xvi, 4–5, 20, 21–30, 21n89, 41–42
symbol of personality, 20n85
systematic method, 80

testimonium spiritus sancti internum, xvi, 15
theologia ad hominem, 64
theological anthropology, 43n54, 60, 87–88
theological exclusivity, 79
theological objectivism, 62n131
theological rationalism, 55–57
theological thinking, 72
theonomic theology, Kutter, 45
theory of consciousness, Schleiermacher, 5, 27
Thielicke, Helmut, 37
"Thinking and Experiencing" (Brunner), 31
Thurneysen, Eduard, 37, 46, 56n104, 77
Tombach lecture, 32n5
transcendence, 12, 16–17, 19–20, 24–27, 28–30, 36, 47
transcendent, participation in, 23, 30
trans-subjective unity, 13, 14, 19, 28
triadic dialectic, 85n51
Troeltsch, Ernst, 60

true and real human, division between, 88
truth, 4–7, 8, 27–28, 40–42, 45, 49–51, 62, 62n131, 82–83, 86, 88, 89–90, 93, 94–95
Truth as Encounter (Brunner), 61, 62, 94
"Truth as Encounter" concept, xvi, 9n25, 107–8
truth of religious knowledge, 4, 6, 27, 30
two kingdoms, Luther's doctrine of, 97

understanding God, 30, 46
unio mystica cum Christo, 15
The Unique and the Character of Existence (Brunner), 68
unity, 17, 26, 28–29
universal spiritual being, 13, 16, 17, 19
"Urbild," Schleiermacher's concept of, 81

verbal ability, xv

Wegscheider, Julius August Ludwig, 51–52, 59
will of God, 35
Windelband, W., 19n78
witness of the Holy Spirit, xvi, 15–16
word-event, 48
word of God, 38, 65–66, 68, 71, 73–76, 80, 94, 96, 99–100
word of revelation, 40, 86
work-based-autonomous ladder to heaven, 38
world experience, 24

Zwischen den Zeiten (magazine), 46